MARK HANKINS

PAUL'S SYSTEM OF TRUTH

THE LIFE AND TEACHINGS
OF THE APOSTLE PAUL

Mark Hankins Ministries
Alexandria, Louisiana
www.markhankins.org

Unless otherwise indicated, all scripture quotations are taken from the *King James Version* of the Bible

Scripture quotations marked AMP are taken from *The Amplified Bible* copyright © 1965, 1987 by Zondervan Corporation.

Scripture quotations marked TLB are taken from *The Living Bible* copyright © 1971 by Tyndale House Publishers, Inc.

Scripture quotations marked MSG are taken from *The Message* copyright © 2002 by NavPress Publishing Group.

Paul's System of Truth
First Edition 2010

Published by
Mark Hankins Ministries
PO Box 12863
Alexandria, LA 71315
www.markhankins.org

Printed in the United States of America.

Table of Contents

O N E

THE LIFE OF PAUL
THE TRAJECTORY OF FAITH

No words of Scripture, if we except those, "God manifest in the flesh," hold within themselves a deeper mystery than this simple formula of the Christian life, "in Christ."
                    - A.J. Gordon

Recently I watched a championship golf match on television. The greatest golfer in the world today stood on the green needing to make a very critical putt. Millions of people watched with millions of dollars at stake.

The golfer walked around the green and viewed the location of the ball from several different angles. He carefully prepared to putt as the crowd watched almost breathlessly. When he hit the ball, it looked like he putted the wrong way! It looked as though he had misjudged the putt and the ball was off course.

1

I was amazed to see the ball turn and head right into the hole. As the crowd cheered, I was shocked that he had made the putt. I thought he had putted the ball the wrong way. However, from my view, I could not see the lay of the land on the green. The golfer actually had to putt the ball uphill. The direction and the pace were critical. He judged it perfectly and the ball landed right in the hole.

As I thought about this, the Lord spoke to me, "I am a champion at *putting* people in the right direction with the perfect pace so that they can fulfill their destiny. When you think I am putting you the wrong way, remember, I can see the lay of the land. I know your strengths and weaknesses. I will perfect that which concerns you, (Psalms 138:8)."

GOD IS A CHAMPION AT "PUTTING" PEOPLE IN THE RIGHT DIRECTION WITH THE PERFECT PACE SO THAT THEY CAN FULFILL THEIR DESTINY.

In this book, we take a look at the life of the Apostle Paul. His life had many unusual turning points but God was perfectly "putting" Paul to his divine calling and destiny. We will see the genius of God as we look at the many turning points in the trajectory of Paul's life. Webster's dictionary defines the word *trajectory* as the path followed by an object moving through space, also a chosen or taken path.

2

Paul's life and ministry are a pattern of how God works in each one of our lives. There is a pattern of mercy, faith, wisdom, grace, truth, and power that we can follow today. As we study the life of Paul and see the heart of Paul in his letters, we will see a "man in Christ." Every man or woman in Christ has a definite trajectory of faith and destiny. When it looks like God is "putting" you the wrong way, remember — He is a Champion. He is able by His Spirit to get you in the right place at the right time to fulfill the call of God on your life.

> *Therefore if any man be in Christ, he is a new creature: old things are passed away; behold, all things are become new.*
>
> *- 2 Corinthians 5:17*

The Apostle Paul refers to himself as a "man in Christ" in 2 Corinthians 12:2. You must understand what Paul means by this phrase a "man in Christ" to understand the epistles. Paul uses the phrases "in Christ," "in Him," and "in Whom" more than 130 times in his writings. He is not only describing his own experience with the Lord Jesus, but also what happens to any man or woman in Christ. Paul's letters are summed up in the following scripture:

3

> *I am crucified with Christ: nevertheless I live; yet*
> *not I, but Christ liveth in me: and the life which I*
> *now live in the flesh I live by the faith of the Son*
> *of God, who loved me, and gave himself for me.*
>
> *- Galatians 2:20*

The reality of Christianity for Paul was, **"...yet not I but Christ liveth in me...."** Jesus is alive, not just in Heaven, but in every believer by the Holy Spirit. Believers are alive not just on the earth, but also in Heaven by virtue of being in Christ. Ephesians 2:6 tells us that God, **"...hath raised us up together, and made us sit together in Heavenly places in Christ Jesus."** Paul's life and ministry are the life of a man in Christ — a happy man.

JESUS IS ALIVE, NOT JUST IN HEAVEN, BUT IN EVERY BELIEVER BY THE HOLY SPIRIT. BELIEVERS ARE ALIVE NOT JUST ON THE EARTH, BUT ALSO IN HEAVEN BY VIRTUE OF BEING IN CHRIST.

If any man be in Christ, he is a new creature. Right now things are turning and moving you in the right direction toward the will of God. Every man in Christ can follow the pattern found in Paul's life. This same pattern will work today to change cities and nations!

There are turning points in every generation. God used Paul, a man in Christ, to revolutionize the thinking and understanding of the leaders of the early church. Paul's letters have endured to influence the church today.

REVOLUTIONS AND TURNING POINTS IN HISTORY

The *U.S. News and World Report* gave this special report on "History's Turning Points" by Daniel Boorstin.

The true watersheds of human affairs are seldom spotted quickly amid the tumult of headlines broadcast on the hour. Overfed on the news, we are in danger of having our sense of history polluted by today's headlines. Today more than ever we need to sharpen our vocabulary and remind ourselves of the differences between history and current events, between "revolution" and the kinds of "turning points" that confuse our view of the latest bulletins. Not until the 17th century did the word "revolution" cease to mean only the circular movement of celestial bodies in their orbits and begin to describe the great "commotions" in society. "Turning points" is a much more recent addition to our vocabulary. The phrase was embraced in the mid-19th century as a way of indicating a sudden change in the direction of things in motion. To move from the wilderness of news into the paths of history, we must distinguish true turning points from mistaken ones. The authentic turning points we call revolutions had centuries old roots.

Words like "revolution" and "turning point" describe the Apostle Paul's impact on history. He definitely caused a great "commotion" in society. Paul caused a sudden change of direction in the early church. He revolutionized the thinking of the early church leaders concerning what happened in the death, burial, and resurrection of Jesus Christ.

As a result, the impact and influence of Christianity went around the world. Paul crossed social, religious, cultural, racial, and geographical boundaries. What God did in Christ was for the whole world and every generation. Paul started a revolution that still shapes and changes the world today. The Lord Jesus Christ used Paul to pioneer the way and to draw the map that believers walk today in Christ.

In his book *Life of Paul*, P.C. Nelson gives a great description of the significance and impact of Paul on Christianity, the world then, and the world now.

> *Great conquerors like Nebuchadnezzar, Alexander the Great, the Caesars, Charlemagne, Canute the Great, Napoleon, and many more have arisen to change the map of the world, but they have passed from the stage of action, and their empires have vanished away. Great philosophers like Pythagoras, Socrates, Plato, Aristotle, Kant, Hegel, Paschal, and many more have appeared, but their teachings and systems are little known except to students of philosophy. Great poets and orators like Homer, Virgil, Cicero, Burke, Webster, and others have come into the lime-light, but they are either unknown to the rank and file of the world, or nearly forgotten. Great explorers, scientists, and statesmen have come and gone, leaving only dim or fading memories. But, this man Paul, who loved to call himself*

a slave — a slave of Jesus Christ — grows larger with the passing centuries, and the legacy he left to the world by far surpasses that left by any of those we have mentioned.

In less than thirty years, by the energy, influence, wisdom, and power of Paul and his associates, Christianity had become a world religion and was firmly established in many great centers, and had taken root even in proud Rome, in the Roman army (Philippians 1:12-18), in the household of Caesar — that human monster, the emperor Nero Caesar (Philippians 4:22) "So mightily grew the word of the Lord and prevailed" (Acts 19:20), not only in Ephesus, but throughout the Roman empire (Romans 15:15-24).

PAUL'S LETTERS DIVINELY INSPIRED, AND RICH IN DEEPEST SPIRITUAL TRUTHS, ARE THE ADVANCED TEACHINGS OF OUR LORD JESUS CHRIST.

Paul was facile princeps (the acknowledged chief; one who stands indisputably first) as a theologian in the apostolic age, and we are still waiting for a clearer thinker and a more profound theologian to arise. In that little bundle of letters, Paul embodied the clearest statement of Christian doctrine extant. He wrote very little himself, but set hundreds of the best scholars in all the Christian centuries to writing to explain and elucidate and amplify the great doctrines, which he delivered to the saints (Jude 3). Enormous libraries might be gathered of books written about Paul, his work and writings. The greatest minds in the Christian ranks have been glad to sit at his feet to learn the way of the Lord more perfectly (Acts 19:26). These letters divinely inspired, and rich in deepest spiritual truths, are the advanced teachings of our Lord Jesus Christ, a necessary and essential part of the Gospel. The four Gospels prepare the way for this further revelation of God's truth, and the Epistles throw a floodlight upon the Gospel records. Peter classes these letters along with "the other scriptures," and admits there are things in them that require study — "Even as our beloved brother Paul also, according to the wisdom given to him, wrote unto you; as also, in all his epistles, speaking in them of these things; wherein are some things hard to be understood, which the ignorant and unsteadfast, wrest, as they do also the other scriptures, unto their destruction" (2 Peter 3:15,16, A.R.V.).

NO GREAT PREACHER HAS ARISEN TO BLESS THE PEOPLE OF GOD WHO HAS NOT LIGHTED HIS TORCH AT THE FLAME KINDLED BY PAUL.

God made Paul a world-preacher for the whole Gospel age. He exercised a powerful influence on the other apostles and other preachers of Apostolic times, and since then no great preacher has arisen to bless the people of God who has not lighted his torch at the flame kindled by Paul. Alas for the cry, "Back to Christ" that is being sounded in the ears of the world today! —Meaning away from Paul and back to the simpler elements of the Gospels. Never! Forward with Paul to Christ! Our Savior is not way back yonder in Palestine and does not lie buried in the tomb of Joseph of Arimathea. "He is risen indeed! And goeth before!" And no better guide than the Apostle Paul can be found to lead us through the mist and darkness of this present evil age, into the very presence of our exalted Lord.

He appears to have all the gifts of the Spirit. We know that he spoke in tongues more than any even in Corinth, where this gift seems to have reached its fullest development (1 Corinthians 14:18); we know that he had discernment for he demonstrated this time and again (Acts 14:8-11). He was a prophet in the highest sense of the word, for many special revelations were given to him (1 Cor. 14:6, 2 Cor. 12:1,7; Gal. 1:12; Romans 16:25,26; Ephesians 3;5). He had divine wisdom (2 Peter 3:15). He had divine knowledge (2 Cor. 11:6; Ephesians 3:4). He was a man of faith — God-given faith (Acts 28:3-6; 27:25). He wrought mighty miracles (Acts 19:11,12). He exercised the gifts of healing (Acts 28:8,9). We are not told that he interpreted messages in tongues, but that goes without saying (1 Cor. 14:13).

Preachers like Chrysostom, Luther, Knox, Wesley, Spurgeon, Finney, Moody, and Gypsy Smith; poets like Tennyson, Whittier, Francis Ridley Harvergal, Fanny Crosby and a host of others owe their finest and highest conceptions to this apostle. Statesmen like Gladstone, David Lloyd George, Daniel Webster, Abraham Lincoln, William Jennings

.

Bryan, and a galaxy of others have laid their tributes at the feet of this man of God. Whole libraries have grown out of the seed thoughts that he sowed. Great universities as well as smaller schools have been planted because this man sent out a blaze of light. Jesus laid the foundation of Gospel truth, supplied the material for the grand superstructure which Paul as a "wise master-builder" erected, He sounds the whole range of divine truth — Theology, Soteriology, Ecclesiology, Eschatology.

PAUL'S WORDS ARE LIVING THINGS WITH HANDS AND FEET.

He was so filled with God that his very words seemed charged with divine power. As Martin Luther expressed it, "His words are living things with hands and feet." He might have added that they grip the heart, enlighten the mind, stir the emotions, engage the conscience and move the will. They probe the soul to its deepest recesses of unsuspected corruption, cleanse and purify its secret festering sores and pour in the balm of Gilead: they speak in thunder tones of impending doom to a Felix, blind the eyes of Elymas, set Aeneas on feet that never before had walked, delivered a slave girl from an oppressing demon of divination and bring cheer to a multitude in time of distress and tempest. Whole sermons may be found in separate words: whole volumes in single sentences. Even after nineteen hundred years, Paul is preaching every week in a thousand languages in a hundred thousand pulpits all over the world.

Paul was the master of every situation. He was indefatigable, inexhaustible, indomitable, and invincible. Unconquerable in life, he was victorious in death.

PAUL'S LETTERS ARE AMONG THE MOST FORCEFUL AND ELOQUENT...IN ALL LITERATURE.

In his article "The Momentous Mission of the Apostle Paul" in *U.S. News and World Report*, Gerald Parshall also describes the undeniable imprint left on the world by Paul.

In the middle years of the first century, preachers of many philosophical stripes *traveled the sea lanes and cobblestone roads of the eastern Roman Empire. Among them was an indefatigable evangelist in a rough coat and crude sandals who supported himself in his missionary work by making tents. Contemporary historians did not deem him worthy of a single mention, having no inkling of how great a tent maker Paul of Tarsus was. They could not know that he was erecting the theological tent to Christianity, making it broad enough to accommodate all manner of humankind, to girdle the globe and to survive two millenniums as a major force in history. He was arrested and driven from one city after another. He was stoned at least once, beaten with rods three times and in five*

WHOLE SERMONS MAY BE FOUND IN SEPARATE WORDS: WHOLE VOLUMES IN SINGLE SENTENCES. EVEN AFTER NINETEEN HUNDRED YEARS, PAUL IS PREACHING EVERY WEEK IN A THOUSAND LANGUAGES IN A HUNDRED THOUSAND PULPITS ALL OVER THE WORLD.

instances given 39 lashes, a punishment that leaves the back a bloody mess and can cause death. While Paul traveled by foot, by donkey, by horseback, and by boat across Asia Minor and Macedonia establishing new congregations, he reinforced his gospel to previous converts with a series of letters that have awed even secular historians. Will Durant called them "among the most forceful and eloquent...in all literature...."

Marvin Wilson, in his book *Did You Know*, also brings to light the importance of the life and letters of the Apostle Paul.

Paul's letters, not the Gospels, give us the earliest information we have about Jesus. All his letters were probably written before the first Gospel was penned. The earliest reference to the sayings of Jesus came from 1 Thessalonians, which Paul wrote about 50 A.D.

THE LIFE OF PAUL
THE TRAJECTORY OF FAITH

Conybeare and Howson give us the principle dates on the chronology of Paul's ministry.

36 A.D.	Conversion
38 A.D.	Flight to Tarsus
44 A.D.	Brought to Antioch by Barnabas
48 A.D.	First Missionary Journey
50 A.D.	Council at Jerusalem
51-54 A.D.	Second Missionary Journey
54-58 A.D.	Third Missionary Journey
57 AD.	1 Corinthians written at Ephesus;
	2 Corinthians in Macedonia;
	Galatians at Corinth
58 A.D.	Romans written at Corinth
59 A.D.	In prison at Caesarea
60 A.D.	Voyage to Rome
62 A.D.	Philemon, Colossians, and
	Ephesians written in Rome
63 A.D.	Release from prison
67 A.D.	1 Timothy and Titus written
68 A.D.	In prison again at Rome.
	2 Timothy. Death

PAUL: A HAPPY MAN

The joy of Jesus strengthened Paul through all adversity. He finished his course with joy and completed the assignment given to him by Jesus Christ (Acts 20:24). In Philippians, one of his last letters, Paul speaks of joy and rejoicing sixteen times in four short chapters. Whatever else a man in Christ is, he is certainly a happy man.

Towards the end of his life, Paul stood before the leaders of the Roman Empire and said, "I think myself happy" (Acts 26:2). Another translation says, "I have been congratulating myself, King Agrippa." Paul was a happy man. If you consider the adversity he encountered in his life, you would expect him to say something different. He could have said, "I am a tired man, a mistreated man, a lonely man, a disappointed man, a hurting man." Instead, Paul described himself as a happy man.

When Paul met Jesus, his whole life and identity changed. He was no longer Saul of Tarsus; he was a new creature. He was not only a changed man, but he was also a different man. His name, identity, and destiny changed. Paul found his new identity in Christ and fulfilled his new destiny. Paul's assignment was to assemble the thoughts given to him by Jesus and publish the message throughout the body of Christ. He was a mouthpiece that Jesus used to speak and write to believers in every generation. This is not only true for Paul, but for any person in Christ. You are such a different person in Christ; you will have to let God introduce you to your new self.

T W O

PAUL'S SYSTEM OF TRUTH

THE POWER OF TRUTH

The Gospel is multi-faceted and meets every need. The four Gospels — Matthew, Mark, Luke, and John — are a proclamation of the Gospel. The book of Acts is a demonstration of the Gospel. Paul's letters are an explanation of the Gospel. The four Gospels are a photograph of redemption. Paul's epistles are an X-ray. An X-ray shows things that cannot be seen in a photograph. In a photo you see the external, but an x-ray shows the internal. Both of these pictures are necessary to see the picture of redemption in its entirety.

THE FOUR GOSPELS ARE A PHOTOGRAPH OF REDEMPTION. PAUL'S EPISTLES ARE AN X-RAY.

Paul's revelation tells the necessity of the crucifixion of Christ. He tells what happened in the unseen — in the spirit realm. The four Gospels tell what man saw. Paul's epistles tell what God saw. He tells what happened when Jesus ascended into Heaven and secured our redemption with His blood.

Paul tells what happened in God's economy when Jesus died and was raised from the dead. Paul's epistles are Jesus, the head of the church, talking to us from the right hand of God. The triumphant, risen Christ is still talking after His resurrection. He speaks to us from His place of victory. He is seated. Redemption is finished.

Paul's letters contain the best explanation of Christianity in the world. James Stalker says:

> *The right way to look at them is to regard them as the continuation of Christ's own teaching. They contain the thoughts that Christ carried away from the world unuttered. Of course Jesus would have stated them differently and far better. Paul's thoughts have everywhere the coloring of his own mental peculiarities. But the substance of them is what Christ's must have been if he had Himself given them expression.*
>
> *There was one great subject especially that Christ had to leave unexplained — His*

own death. He could not explain it before it had taken place. This became the leading topic of Paul's thinking — to show why it was needed and what were its blessed results.

THE RIGHT WAY TO LOOK AT PAUL'S LETTERS IS TO REGARD THEM AS THE CONTINUATION OF CHRIST'S OWN TEACHING. THEY CONTAIN THE THOUGHTS THAT CHRIST CARRIED AWAY FROM THE WORLD UNUTTERED.

But there was no aspect of the appearance of Christ into which his restlessly inquiring mind was constantly getting deeper and deeper into the subject. The progress of his thinking was determined partly by the natural progress of his own advance in the knowledge of Christ, for he always wrote out of his own experience; and partly by the various forms of error that he had at successive periods encountered, and which became a providential means of stimulating and developing his apprehension of the truth, just as ever since in the Christian church the rise of error has been the means of calling forth the clearest statements of doctrine. The ruling impulse, however, of his thinking, as of his life, was ever Christ, and it was his lifelong devotion to this exhaustless theme that made him the thinker of Christianity.

To get anywhere in life you need a point of reference, a landmark. Several years ago while in Paris, France, I couldn't figure out which way the streets were going because they don't make blocks. What really helped me was to see an aerial view of the city. From above I could see that the streets of the city were like spokes on a bicycle wheel. The spokes came to the center of the city at the Arc of Triumph.

I realized that if I knew where I was in relation to the Arc of Triumph, the center of the city, I could figure out where the restaurants, museums, river, or the Louvre were from this landmark. You need to have a few landmarks to get around in Paris.

Sometimes life can get pretty complicated. The devil brings thoughts and imaginations. You go through trials and difficulties. No matter what trouble you are facing in life, if you can find the Arc of Triumph — the Gospel — and get back to your redemption, you can get anywhere you need to go from there. The center of the Gospel is what

God has done for you in Christ in His death, burial, and resurrection. That is the center of Paul's system of truth; it is what God has already accomplished for you. Redemption is an accomplished fact in the mind of God. The Gospel is not what you are trying to get God to do for you — it is what God has already done for you.

A BETTER SYSTEM

Hold fast the form of sound words, which thou hast heard of me, in faith and love which is in Christ Jesus.

- 2 Timothy 1:13

Hold fast and follow the pattern of wholesome and sound teaching which you have heard from me, in [all] the faith and love which are [for us] in Christ Jesus.

- Amplified Bible

Hold tightly to the pattern of truth I taught you, especially concerning the faith and love Christ Jesus offers you.

- Living Bible

And the Holy Spirit uses all this to point out to us that under the old system the common people could not go into the Holy of Holies as long as the outer room and the entire system it represents were still in use. This has an important lesson for us today. For under the old system, gifts and sacrifices were offered, but these failed to cleanse the hearts of the people who brought them. For the old system dealt only with certain rituals — what foods to eat and drink, rules for washing themselves, and rules about this and that. The people had to keep these rules to tide them over until Christ came with God's new and better way. He came as High Priest of this better system which we now have. He went into that greater, perfect tabernacle in heaven, not made by men nor part of this world, and once for all took blood into that inner room, the Holy of Holies, and sprinkled it on the mercy seat; but it was not the blood of goats and calves. No, he took his own blood, and with it he, by himself, made sure of our eternal salvation. And if under the old system the blood of bulls and goats and the ashes of young cows could cleanse men's bodies from sin, just think how much more surely the blood of Christ will transform our lives and hearts. His sacrifice frees us from the worry of having to obey the

old rules, and makes us want to serve the living
God. For by the help of the eternal Holy Spirit,
Christ willingly gave himself to God to die for
our sins — he being perfect, without a single sin
or fault.

- Hebrews 9:8-14 - Living Bible

The writer of Hebrews wanted to explain that the old laws cannot compare to the work of redemption that God has done for us in Christ. Apparently, many Jewish Christians were thinking of turning from their new life of faith in Christ who mediated a better covenant and offered a better sacrifice for us.

The <u>old system</u> of Jewish laws gave only a dim
foretaste of the good things Christ would do for
us. The sacrifices under the <u>old system</u> were
repeated again and again, year after year, but
even so they could never save those who lived
under their rules. If they could have, one offering
would have been enough; the worshippers would
have been cleansed once for all, and their feeling
of guilt would be gone...After Christ said this,
about not being satisfied with the various
sacrifices and offerings required under the <u>old</u>
<u>system</u>, he then added, "Here I am. I have come

25

> *to give my life." He cancels the <u>first system</u> in favor of a far better one. Under this new plan we have been forgiven and made clean by Christ's dying for us once and for all.*
>
> *- Hebrews 10:1-3, 9, 10 - Living Bible*

The first system had to be replaced by a new and better system so man could have fellowship with God. If you were still living under the old system you would have to bring animals to be sacrificed for forgiveness. Each time you sinned, you would be required to bring a blood sacrifice to church, just like they had to do in the Old Testament. We no longer have to do that. The old system was done away with. The first system that was established has been replaced with a new and better system ordained by God and sealed by the blood of His Son, Jesus Christ.

THE OLD SYSTEM WAS DONE AWAY WITH AND HAS BEEN REPLACED BY A NEW SYSTEM.

Whatever Paul taught in Rome, he also taught in Colossae, Ephesus, Corinth, Thessalonica, and also wrote to the Hebrews. Paul's letters contain a system of truth that enables the believer to understand and grow in the reality of what Jesus has done and is doing for us.

I like the way James Stalker said, "Paul's letters contain the thoughts that Jesus carried away from this world unuttered." Jesus had so much more to tell his disciples that he could not tell them while he was on earth (John 16:12-15). He had to wait until after His death, burial, and resurrection to tell them.

Paul's revelation is for every believer. You should read the book of Ephesians like Jesus is writing you a letter through the Apostle Paul. There is a powerful revelation of truth in these letters. There is a system of truth that sets you free — free indeed!

> *But God be thanked, that ye were the servants of sin, but ye have obeyed from the heart that form of doctrine which was delivered you.*
>
> *- Romans 6:17*

> *But thanks be to God that though you were once in thralldom to sin, you have now yielded a hearty obedience to that SYSTEM OF TRUTH in which you were instructed.*
>
> *- Weymouth*

> *Thank God! Your thralldom to sin is a thing of the past: you have rendered allegiance — from the heart you have rendered it — to the New Teaching, the mold into which you have let your nature berun.*
>
> *- Way*

27

The *King James Version* calls it a "form of doctrine." *Way's* translation calls it the "new teaching." *Rotherham's* translation calls it the "mold of teaching." My favorite is *Weymouth's* translation: **"...that system of truth in which you were instructed."** Paul's "system of truth" can be found throughout his epistles. This system is powerful.

> *...you shall know the truth and the truth shall make you free...If the Son therefore shall make you free, you shall be free indeed.*
>
> *- John 8:32, 36*

Since Satan is a liar, the truth would do great damage to him. There is tremendous power in truth. The truth is in Jesus. The truth is in the Word of God. The Holy Spirit is called the Spirit of truth (John 16:13). In this book, we will take a journey through Paul's System of Truth. This system of truth broke the control of sin and Satan and set the believer free to serve God.

> *Being then made free from sin, you became the servants of righteousness.*
>
> *- Romans 6:18*

JESUS SAID YOU SHALL KNOW THE TRUTH AND THE TRUTH SHALL MAKE YOU FREE. PAUL'S SYSTEM OF TRUTH BROKE THE CONTROL OF SIN AND SATAN AND SET THE BELIEVER FREE TO SERVE GOD.

THE NEW SYSTEM OF TRUTH

The new system of truth was necessary because of the death, burial, and resurrection of Christ. Jesus didn't go through the agony of the crucifixion, the suffering of the cross, and the glory or His resurrection without effecting radical change. The death, burial, and resurrection of Christ changed everything.

> *Therefore if any man be in Christ, he is a new creature: old things are passed away; behold all things are become new.*
>
> *- 2 Corinthians 5:17*

Noah Webster's Dictionary 1828 gives us a working definition for the words "system" and "systematical."

SYSTEM: An assemblage of things adjusted into a regular whole; or a whole plan or scheme consisting of many parts connected in such a manner as to create a chain of mutual dependencies; or a regular union of principles or parts forming one entire thing. Thus we say a system of logic, a system of philosophy, a system of government, a system of principles, the solar system....

29

<u>SYSTEMATICAL:</u> Formed with regular connection and adaptation or subordination of parts to each other, and to design the whole.

One of the simplest illustrations of a system is a chain. A chain is a group of links that are interdependent upon each other for the strength of the whole. Not any one link can be a chain; all the links are dependent upon the other.

The Apostle Paul's letters contain an inter-dependent group of revelation realities that came from what God has done for us in Christ. This system of truth centers on the death, burial, and resurrection of Christ with the restoration of man as the object. In Paul's System of Truth, the eight points are the eight links, which have their center in redemption. In Paul's revelation we understand the Bible in the light of redemption. We also learn to see our personal lives in the light of redemption.

> *Who hath delivered us from the power of darkness, and hath translated us into the kingdom of his dear Son.*
>
> *- Colossians 1:13*

Satan can only operate as "a power of darkness." His works can only succeed in the dark. So the light of the Gospel of Christ stops anything that only works in the dark.

Without an understanding of these principles, you will be spiritually handicapped. It is not who you are in yourself or your abilities that matter; it is who you are because you have been born again and are in union with Christ. This is the bottom line of your faith — the network or system from which everything you do in your Christian walk must center. This is Paul's System of Truth.

THE 8 POINTS OF PAUL'S SYSTEM OF TRUTH

1. Paul's Pneuma Concept: Spirit, Soul, and Body

2. Identification with Adam

3. Man's Condition in Adam

4. What Happened to Jesus —
   From the Cross to the Throne

5. Identification with Christ

6. Who we are and What we have Now in Christ

7. What Jesus is Doing for us Now

8. How to Grow Up in Christ

THREE

PAUL'S PNEUMA CONCEPT
System of Truth — Point One

PLANT OR ANIMAL?

Science classifies all living things in two categories: plants or animals. Scientists have put man in the animal kingdom. One day my high school biology teacher asked the class, "How many of you are plants?" No one raised a hand. He asked, "How many of you are animals?" Some students raised their hands; others did not. He asked if anyone in the class was dead. He kept on and on in an effort to make his point — that every living thing is either plant or animal.

My teacher continued until everyone in the class had raised a hand except me. He asked me, "Are you a plant?" I said, "No, I am not a plant." Then he asked me, "Are you an animal?" I said, "No, I am not an animal." He asked, "What are you, then?" I answered, "I am a spirit made in the image of God, made a shade lower than God Himself." He looked at me and said, "I am not talking about church." I told him, "I am not talking about church, either."

THE SPIRIT DIMENSION: ANOTHER KINGDOM

Jesus said He would tell us about another kingdom — an unseen kingdom. Other translators call it the "realm of God" and the "dominion of God." Jesus said, **"I am come that you might have life and have it more abundantly," (John 10:10).**

The world only recognizes the plant and animal kingdoms. You are not meant to operate like an animal and be caught up in the "seen" world. You are a spirit made in God's image. When you are born again, you receive eternal life and move into a new kingdom. You receive the life of God in your spirit and become a part of the kingdom of God.

WHAT IS MAN?

What is man, that thou art mindful of him? And the son of man that thou visitest him? For thou hast made him a little lower than the angels, and hast crowned him with glory and honour. Thou madest him to have dominion over the works of thy hands; thou hast put all things under his feet.

- Psalm 8:4-6

Man did not evolve from a monkey. In fact, Psalm 8 says that God made man a little lower than the angels. The word for angels in this scripture is "Elohim" or God. Man is made a shade lower than God Himself.

In Genesis 1:26 God said, **"Let us make man in our image, after our likeness...."** Not only is man made in the image of God, but he is also created to have dominion over the works of God's hands. Man functions the way God functions. The works of the enemy have been put under his feet through the work of Christ.

SPIRIT, SOUL, AND BODY

And the very God of peace sanctify you wholly; and I pray God your whole spirit and soul and body be preserved blameless unto the coming of our Lord Jesus Christ.

- 1 Thessalonians 5:23

Created in the image of God, man is a spirit, who has a soul, and resides in a body. This does not mean you are one-third spirit, one-third soul, and one-third body. More accurately, you can say of yourself, "I am a spirit, I have a soul, and I live in a body."

GOD IS FATHER PNEUMA; HE MADE PEOPLE TO BE LITTLE PNEUMAS.

PAUL'S PNEUMA CONCEPT

The Greek word for "spirit" is *pneuma*. John 4:24 says, **"God is a Spirit: and they that worship him must worship him in spirit and in truth."** Jesus said God is a Spirit or *Pneuma*. Since man is made in the image of God, man is also a spirit or *pneuma*.

> *Furthermore we have had fathers of our flesh which corrected us, and we gave them reverence: shall we not much rather be in subjection unto the Father of spirits, and live?*
>
> *- Hebrews 12:9*

In this scripture, God is called Father of Spirits or He is the "Father of pneumas." You are a spirit, with a soul (which includes your mind, will, and emotions), and you are staying in a body (the house you live in). Many theologians have said, "We cannot understand Paul's letters. We know that people have a mind and a body, but what is this pneuma concept?"

PAUL'S LETTERS ARE CENTERED ON THE TRUTH THAT MAN IS A SPIRIT BEING.

Paul's pneuma concept embraces the realm of the Spirit. Man is a spirit; he is connected to God. God is a

Spirit. God is a Pneuma, and man is a pneuma. I like to say it this way: God is Father Pneuma; He made people to be little pneumas. The Holy Spirit bears witness with our pneuma that we are the children of God (Romans 8:16). The big "Pneuma" bears witness with the little pneumas.

> *For as many as are led by the Spirit of God, they*
> *are the sons of God.*
>
> > *- Romans 8:14*

MAN IS A PNEUMA BEING

When God (Father Pneuma) formed Adam's body and breathed into him, He inhaled in Heaven and exhaled into Adam (Genesis 2:7). When Adam stood up, he walked and talked like Father Pneuma. He had pneuma love, pneuma glory, pneuma honor, and he exercised pneuma dominion. Adam's mind was so sharp because he was in fellowship with God, Father Pneuma. Without trying to think up new words, he named all the animals.

Adam was not a cave man. He walked and talked with God in the cool of the day. God said, "I want to talk to My man." Father Pneuma talked with little pneuma.

> *And God said, Let us make man in our image,*
> *after our likeness: and let them have*
> *dominion....*
>
> > *- Genesis 1:26*

37

ADAM'S PNEUMA DEATH

The devil hated Adam because Adam looked like God. Adam had everything that comes from walking with God in the realm of the Spirit. He was a happy man. The devil knew if Adam sinned, he would die spiritually and lose his dominion, love, joy, and peace. The devil knew he could mess man up totally if he died spiritually.

When God made Adam, He originally gave him a body that would live forever. The day Adam sinned, he died spiritually. His spirit was cut off from fellowship with God. His spirit, soul, and body remained intact. His soul and his body took the ascendancy, and his human nature took control of him. His spirit was bound and gagged and unable to function.

In Adam we are also spiritually dead, or separated from God. This leaves the door open to the devil. Satan controls a spiritually dead person through his flesh and his mind. If you are not born again, your spirit is not hooked up to God. You are spiritually dead. A person who is not born again can develop his spirit; however, the only way he can is to get hooked up with unclean or familiar spirits in the spirit realm.

Paul's letters are centered on the fact that the real you is a spirit not a body. If Adam had never sinned, it would not be necessary for Paul's revelation to divide spirit, soul, and body.

James Stalker gives keen insight of Paul's pneuma concept in *The Life of St. Paul*:

> *The nature of man, according to Paul, normally consists of three sections — body, soul, and spirit. In his original constitution these occupied definite relations of superiority and subordination to one another, the spirit being supreme, the body least important, and the soul occupying the middle position.*

CHRIST RESTORES THE LOST PREDOMINANCE OF THE SPIRIT OF MAN BY TAKING POSSESSION OF IT BY HIS OWN SPIRIT.

> *But the Fall disarranged this order, and all sin consists in the usurpation by the body or the soul of the place of the spirit. In fallen man these two inferior sections of human nature, which together form what Paul calls the "flesh," or that side of human nature that looks toward the world and time, have taken possession of the throne and completely rule the life, while the spirit, the side of man that*

looks toward God and eternity, has been dethroned and reduced to a condition of inefficiency and death. Christ restores the lost predominance of the spirit of man by taking possession of it by His own Spirit. His Spirit dwells in the human spirit, vivifying it and sustaining it in such growing strength that it becomes more and more the sovereign part of the human constitution. The man ceases to be carnal and becomes spiritual; he is led by the Spirit of God and becomes more and more harmonious with all that is holy and divine.

The flesh does not, indeed, easily submit to the loss of supremacy. It clogs and obstructs the spirit and fights to regain possession of the throne. Paul has described this struggle in sentences of stark vividness, in which all generations of Christians have recognized the features of their deepest experience. But the issue of the struggle is not doubtful. Sin shall not again have dominion over those in whom Christ's Spirit dwells, or dislodge them from their standing in the favor of God.

STEPPING INTO A NEW WORLD

When you are born again or saved, your pneuma (spirit) is born again, hooked up to God (Romans 8:2). You step out of one world and step into another.

Who hath delivered us from the power of darkness, and hath translated us into the kingdom of his dear Son.

- Colossians 1:13

It was the Father who sprang us from the jail house of darkness, and turned us loose in the New World of His Beloved Son.

- Jordan

When anyone is united to Christ, there is a new world; the old order has gone, and a new order has already begun.

- 2 Corinthians 5:17 - New English Bible

If anyone has entered into fellowship with Christ, a new world has at once opened upon him, an old world has passed away.

- Stanley

41

GET PNEUMATIZED!

The new birth is the circumcision of the heart. Your heart and your spirit are synonymous terms. When Paul talked about "with the heart," he was talking about your spirit, the hidden man of the heart.

> *For we are the circumcision, which worship God in the spirit, and rejoice in Christ Jesus, and have no confidence in the flesh.*
>
> *- Philippians 3:3*

Paul said that those who are born of God are children of God, whether Jew or Gentile. Whether there is an outward sign of circumcision or not, they will worship God in the Spirit and have no confidence in the flesh. We worship God in the pneuma. Paul said, "I serve God in the pneuma."

> *Because the carnal mind is enmity against God: for it is not subject to the law of God, neither indeed can be.*
>
> *- Romans 8:7*

Your mind must be set on spirit or pneuma things. Your mind needs to get pneumatized! You get your clothes martinized (dry cleaned), so you ought to get your mind

42

pneumatized! You can take the realities of the realm of the Spirit and who you are in the Spirit and *pneumatize* your mind.

PAUL SAID YOU ARE MADE UP OF THREE PARTS: SPIRIT, SOUL, AND BODY.

EXERCISE PNEUMA AUTHORITY

The dominion that God gave to Adam was conditional. His spirit had to stay in fellowship with God. When Adam's spirit died, he lost his dominion. Man is a spirit, and his dominion comes from his spirit or *pneuma*.

When we are born again, dominion is restored to us. Our dominion functions through our spirit, or inward man. You will not exercise dominion in this world through your flesh or your mind. The power and authority of God will be exercised through your spirit dominated by the Holy Spirit.

FEED YOUR PNEUMA THE WORD

Your soul (mind, will, emotions) and your spirit are so close together that you can hardly tell them apart. The Scripture says that only the Word of God can separate and divide between your soul and your spirit (Hebrews 4:12).

43

Only when you are filled with the Holy Ghost, spending time in the Word, and in the presence of God can you distinctly tell the difference between your spirit and your soul. Your spirit is the part of you that is most like God. As the Word feeds your spirit, your inward man will rise up and take dominion over your body and mind.

THE UNSEEN REALM AND THE NATURAL MAN

In the unseen realm of the Spirit, your spirit man, the unseen part of you, hooks up to the realm of God. You begin to see who you are in Christ — who God says you are. As your spirit takes hold and begins to feed on the Word, the unseen part of you begins to dominate the seen.

Paul said you are made up of three parts: spirit, soul, and body. Each of these three distinct parts has a function. In Greek, the word for "spirit" is *pneuma*, the word for "soul" is *psuche,* and the word for "body" is *soma*.

> *But the natural man receiveth not the things of the Spirit of God: for they are foolishness unto him: neither can he know them, because they are spiritually discerned.*
>
> *- 1 Corinthians 2:14*

The natural man, the *psuche* man, does not understand the things of the Spirit of God — they do not make sense to him. He cannot know them because they are spiritually (*pneuma*) discerned.

The natural man is like a person who does not have a radio, yet the key to his future and to his life is in the radio waves in the air. People say they do not believe in the unseen, but they use the unseen every day just by turning on the radio. The natural man does not receive the things of the Spirit of God, for they are foolishness to him.

WHICH CHANNEL ARE YOU ON?

The natural man has his radio set on the *psuche* (soul) channel, which is the mind, reasoning, and emotions. He has his mind set on the things that are seen. He is not receiving anything from the *pneuma* channel because he has the dial set on the *psuche* channel.

Some people live their entire life on either the *psuche* (soul) channel or on the *soma* (body or flesh) channel. If they are on the soul channel, they will receive everything through their reasoning or their emotions. If they are on the flesh channel, they will receive everything through their desires, feelings, urges, and needs. These channels will broadcast trash to you.

45

The *soma* (flesh) channel can overwhelm the *psuche* (soul) channel. You think you are in control of your life and suddenly, your flesh controls you. You do things you cannot understand. Suggestions, ideas, and pressures come against you from the *soma* and the *psuche* channels.

When you are born again, God says, "Let me show you another channel — the *pneuma* channel." On this channel you hear that Christ has redeemed you.

> *The law of the Spirit of life in Christ Jesus has made me free from the law of sin and death.*
>
> *- Romans 8:2*

The *pneuma* channel broadcasts songs of deliverance and redemption and songs about your righteousness in Christ. Your Bible shows you everything that is on *pneuma* channel. Everything you need for life and godliness is written in the Word.

THE PNEUMA CHANNEL BROADCASTS SONGS OF DELIVERANCE AND REDEMPTION AND SONGS ABOUT YOUR RIGHTEOUSNESS IN CHRIST.

SOUL POWER

Psuche, the Greek word for "soul" is where we get the word "psychosomatic." The mind, or soul, can have

46

awesome power over the body. This simply means that what you are thinking affects your body. A psychosomatic illness originates in the soul and affects the body. Professionals cannot just treat your body. They have to persuade you to change your way of thinking as well. When you have a psychosomatic illness, the doctor may give you a sugar pill to make you think your body is being treated. The challenge is actually in your mind.

YOUR SPIRIT HAS AN IMPACT ON YOUR SOUL.

You can develop your soul (your mind, will, and emotions) to a degree where it exercises authority over your body. Psychologists have proven this fact. Ulcers and stress have proven this. To some degree your mind is more powerful than your body.

> *Because the carnal mind is enmity against God:*
> *for it is not subject to the law of God, neither*
> *indeed can be.*
>
> *- Romans 8:7*

If it is possible to have a psychosomatic illness, then it must be possible to have a *"pneuma*-somatic" healing. If it is possible that the *psuche* (the soul or mind) can have an effect on the body, then it must be possible that the *pneuma* (the spirit) can have an effect on the body.

47

If the soul is more powerful than the body, and the spirit is more powerful than the soul or mind, that must mean it is possible to have a "*pneuma-psuche*" change. Your spirit has an impact on your soul. Instead of your soul (mind) dominating your life with confusion, worry, and anxiety, your inner man (your spirit — the part of you that is most like God) gets in union with Christ.

WHAT IS TRUE ABOUT YOU IN CHRIST IS TRUE ABOUT YOU SPIRITUALLY.

Jesus feeds your spirit when you are in union with His Spirit — like being hooked up to a feeding tube. Your spirit rises up and takes authority over your soul (your mind, will, and emotions). Your values, philosophies, and thinking will change and have an effect on your body.

> *For they that are after the flesh do mind the things of the flesh; but they that are after the Spirit, the things of the Spirit. For to be carnally minded is death; but to be spiritually minded is life and peace.*
>
> - *Romans 8:5,6*

God's method of salvation works from the inside out through grace. Salvation begins by spiritually being put in

48

union with Christ. Through this union He feeds you with everything necessary not only for you to experience complete salvation and sanctification, but also to meet all your needs.

SANCTIFIED FROM THE INSIDE OUT

Therefore if any man be in Christ he is a new creature: old things are passed away; behold all things are become new.

- 2 Corinthians 5:17

What is true about you in Christ is true about you spiritually. You do not become a new creation physically in your body because you still have the same body. You do not become a new creation mentally because even after you are saved, you continue to have problems with your mind. That means your mind did not pass away. You became brand-new in your spirit. First Corinthians 6:17 seals it for you, **"But he that is joined unto the Lord is one spirit."**

In his letters, Paul took all that God has done for you in Christ, explained what Jesus is doing for you now, and showed your identification in Christ. The Spirit of God is working and living on the inside of you. Paul said that God is sanctifying you wholly — spirit, soul, and body (1 Thessalonians 5:23). God is working on you from the inside to the outside. You must renew your mind and consecrate your body to the service of righteousness by getting your body to work, move, and respond in righteousness.

> *I beseech you therefore, brethren, by the mercies of God, that ye present your bodies a living sacrifice, holy, acceptable unto God, which is your reasonable service. And be not conformed to this world: but be ye transformed by the renewing of your mind....*
>
> *- Romans 12:1,2*

It is your reasonable service to present your body to God and not to allow the values, thinking, philosophies, direction, pressures, spirit, or people of this world to shape you.

THE SPIRIT VS. THE FLESH

Years ago, a study was done to determine the value of a human body. The research concluded that the body is worth eighty-six cents. With inflation, your body would probably be worth about $2.00 today! Are you going to let $2.00 worth of dirt control your life?

Your body will say, "I am not going to pray." You say, "Okay, I'm not praying." The body says, "I am not going to study the Word." You say, "All right, I'm not going to do it because I don't feel like it. I am not going to church either because I don't feel like it." Your body may say, "I am offended. They did not treat me right." You need to get a bulldozer and get your two dollars worth of dirt moving in the right direction!

> *Know ye not that they which run in a race run all, but one receiveth the prize? So run, that ye may obtain. And every man that striveth for the mastery is temperate in all things. Now they do it to obtain a corruptible crown; but we an incorruptible. I therefore so run, not as uncertainly; so fight I, not as one that beateth the air. But I keep under my body, and bring it into subjection lest that by any means, when I have preached to others, I myself should be a castaway.*
>
> *- 1 Corinthians 9:24-27*

The word *castaway* is the same Greek word for *disqualified*. Paul said if you do not keep your body under subjection, you will be disqualified. You will not be able to

51

finish. If Paul had a chance to be disqualified, do you think you and I have a chance to be disqualified? You may think, "I am so important in the kingdom of God I could never be disqualified!" Paul was the head of the whole Gentile church, yet he said he could be disqualified.

Paul ascended to the third Heaven, talked to Jesus, and heard words unlawful for man to utter. He received divine revelation and wrote two-thirds of the New Testament. If Paul had all that revelation and still needed to keep under his body and bring it into subjection, then you and I will need to keep our bodies in subjection to the Holy Spirit.

GOD HAS TAKEN CARE OF YOUR REDEMPTION, BUT YOU HAVE TO DO SOMETHING WITH YOUR BODY AND YOUR MIND.

Paul said that he told his body what to do. He did not allow his body to do what it wanted to do. In Colossians 3:5, Paul said, "Mortify therefore your members which are upon the earth." In Romans 8:13 he said, "For if ye live after the flesh, ye shall die: but if ye through the Spirit do mortify the deeds of the body, ye shall live."

God has taken care of your redemption, but *you* have to do something with *your* body and *your* mind. As long as you are in this world, you will never get to the place where you do not have trouble with your body. Paul called it a war between your spirit and your flesh.

THE INWARD MAN

Paul gave us a good definition of the inward man and the outward man when he said, "*I* (the man on the inside) keep under my body, and *I* (the man on the inside) bring *it* (the body) into subjection." When you are born again, your spirit (inward man) is joined to Christ and becomes a new creation.

> *For which cause we faint not; but though our outward man perish, yet the inward man is renewed day by day.*
>
> *- 2 Corinthians 4:16*

Paul said that although his outward man goes through affliction and difficulty, his inward man is being renewed daily. He spoke of the conflict between the flesh (the outward man) and the spirit (the inward man). He said, "Renewal, restoration, and strengthening is happening in my inward man every day."

THE SPIRIT OF MAN IS WHAT MAKES HIM DIFFERENT FROM EVERY OTHER CREATED BEING.

Your spirit is not just a mist or a vapor on the inside of you. Peter calls your spirit "the hidden man of the heart," and Paul calls your spirit "the inward man." You are a spirit, you have a soul, and you live in a body. Your spirit and your soul together make up the inward man.

Man is a spirit, he has a soul, and he lives in a body. The spirit of man — the part of man that is most like God is eternal. The spirit of man is what makes him different from every other created being.

This truth is essential to the remaining seven points in Paul's System of Truth. The Apostle Paul's writings can only be comprehended by understanding that you are an eternal being made in the image of God not just the body that houses your inward man. God expects *you* to get *your* body and soul in subjection to your spirit man by availing yourself to His Holy Spirit and His Word.

PNEUMA REFERENCES

John 4:23,24	God is a Spirit — Pneuma
Romans 8:2	The law of the spirit of life in Christ Jesus — Pneuma life
Romans 8:4	The Pneuma walk
Romans 8:5,6	The Pneuma mind
Romans 8:9	In the Spirit (Pneuma)

Romans 8:10	The spirit of man is alive
Romans 8:14	Sons of God - led by the Pneuma of God
Romans 5:5	Pneuma love
Romans 2:28,29	The new birth, spiritual circumcision, in the spirit
Romans 1:9	Worship in the Pneuma
Romans 10:8-10	Pneuma faith
Ephesians 1:3	Pneuma blessing
Ephesians 1:17	Pneuma wisdom and revelation
Ephesians 2:4-6	Pneuma love, life, dominion
Ephesians 6:17	Pneuma sword — the Word of God
Galatians 5:16	Walk in the Pneuma
Galatians 5:18	Led, directed by the Pneuma
Galatians 5:22-23	The fruit of the Pneuma
Galatians 5:25	Live and walk in the spirit (pneuma)
Galatians 6:8	Sowing and reaping from the Pneuma
1 Timothy 4:8	Pneuma exercise
2 Timothy 1:7	Pneuma power, love, and a sound mind
1 Corinthians 2:9-14	Pneuma channel - reception, speaking, understanding
1 Corinthians 12:1-10	Pneuma gifts and manifestations
1 Corinthians 14:2	Praying in the Spirit (Pneuma) speaking divine secrets
1 Corinthians 14:14	My spirit (pneuma) prays
1 Corinthians 14:15	My spirit sings - pneuma singing

Hebrews 12:9	Father of spirits - Daddy Pneuma
John 5:24,25	Pneuma Life
John 6:63	Pneuma words
Mark 11:23	Pneuma words and authority
1 Corinthians 6:17	Joined to Jesus — joined at the Pneuma

F O U R

MAN'S IDENTIFICATION WITH ADAM
System of Truth — Point Two

BEFORE YOU WERE BORN

If your parents moved to Louisiana from Texas before you were born, their choice would affect the state you were born in. You would not be a Texan; you would be a Louisianan. Why? Yet unborn, you were in your parents when they moved whether they knew it or not. When they moved, their decision affected you.

Parents often make decisions that affect the way their children are born and the way they are raised. They make decisions that have certain results that are passed on. Many times people think when they disobey God their disobedience only affects them. Their disobedience really affects their families and those future generations in them.

Everyone in the entire human race originated from the Garden of Eden out of the first man, Adam, and his wife,

Eve. Your nationality, where you live, or what language you speak does not matter. You could not have come into this earth any other way except through Adam's lineage.

God created Adam in a state of righteousness and holiness. Adam had direct, personal fellowship with God and had dominion over the works of God's hands. God crowned Adam and Eve with glory and honor, blessed them and gave them a wonderful spirit, intellect (soul), and body. God made them just the way He wanted everyone to be — blessed, happy, victorious, and prosperous.

YOU WERE NOT BORN IN THE CONDITION ADAM WAS CREATED IN; YOU WERE BORN IN THE CONDITION HE PASSED ON.

When Adam sinned, he passed from fellowship with God — from life to death. You were not born in the condition Adam was created in; you were born in the condition he *passed on*. Through Adam — through one man's disobedience — we were all affected.

ADAM WAS NOT DECEIVED

We understand from scripture that the serpent deceived Eve. When the Lord asked her what she had done, she told him, "**...The serpent beguiled me, and I did eat" (Genesis 3:13).** Yet, it was not really Eve's sin that affected the whole human race; Adam's sin did. Adam was not deceived. Adam knew exactly what he was doing when he disobeyed God. Adam knew the moment he took of the fruit of that tree, spiritual death would set in. He knew he would lose his authority and it would affect the entire human race.

When God judged Adam and Eve, He judged them differently. Adam knew what he was doing and carried the responsibility as head of the family. Notice that God first asked Adam what happened.

Adam's job was actually to guard the garden, take dominion, and keep the devil out. Adam reneged on his authority and allowed his wife to be in a place she should not have been to listen to the devil. When God confronted him with his failure, Adam tried to blame everyone but himself. He replied, **"The *woman* whom *thou* gavest to be with me, she gave me of the tree, and I did eat" (Genesis 3:12).** Ultimately, Adam's negligence and disobedience caused man to lose his dominion.

ADAM, THE ARCHETYPE OF MANKIND

In our offices we have different kinds of copiers. We make copies of paper, cassette tapes, video tapes, and now cd's and dvd's. To make copies of cassette tapes, we have one machine with a place that says, "Master." The other places on the machine say "copy." You can make one copy of the master or duplicate hundreds of copies.

In every case, the same material on the master is duplicated onto the copies whether we make 2 copies or 100 copies. The same defects, sounds, or information that are on the master are duplicated identically onto the copies. If the master is bad, the copies are bad. If the master is good, the copies are good.

Adam was more than just one man. Adam was an archetype or the "master." God did not create the entire human race at once. He created one man and one woman and gave them the capacity of procreation. God let Adam father His family.

God put in Adam everything the whole human race could want — joy, blessing, and dominion. God made him the "master." Adam and Eve had all these things. God called them man and woman and the two together had dominion.

When Adam sinned, the "master" developed a defect. Sin, sickness, death, depression, and confusion — every kind of defect you can imagine — marred the master. Adam and Eve began to reproduce and make copies. Those copies went all over the world throughout the history of man. One man messed up the whole thing. We were born, not in the condition that God created Adam, but in the condition caused by Adam's sin. Adam, now a blemished master, produced and duplicated the same blemish in every copy that was ever born.

A COPY OF THE MASTER

What was God going to do with these millions and millions of bad copies? Satan thought he had won, but God had a plan from the foundation of the world. God did some genetic engineering and made a new master. God could do this because He is the Creator. He allowed His only Son to become a man, born of a woman, conceived by the Holy Spirit.

God was manifested in the flesh and walked the earth with us. Jesus came for three reasons: to reveal the goodness of God, to destroy the works of the devil, and to redeem us to God through the cross.

When you are born again, you get on another machine. You get off the Adam machine and onto Christ's machine. Christ is the "master" now. When you get on His machine, the power of His death erases your old condition.

The power of His resurrection identifies you with a whole new humanity, a whole new creation. You are not the same person anymore. You no longer identify only with your natural family. You are now identified with Christ (Point 5 in *Paul's System of Truth*).

The same law that allowed one man to affect every man is the same law that allowed Jesus Christ, the last Adam, to take the first Adam's condition of sin, the curse, shame, and death.

IDENTIFIED WITH ADAM

Wherefore, as by one man sin entered into the world, and death by sin; and so death passed upon all men, for that all have sinned.

- Romans 5:12

Mankind is in the condition that Adam passed into when he sinned in the Garden of Eden. One man, Adam, affected the entire human race. Through one man's disobedience all were made sinners (Romans 5:17). The whole Bible is really about two men: the first Adam and the last Adam. You get your sin nature from the first Adam, which Paul refers to as the old man. The "new man" is Christ who is called the last Adam.

THE WHOLE BIBLE IS REALLY ABOUT TWO MEN: THE FIRST ADAM AND THE LAST ADAM.

Man's condition cannot be corrected by reading a book or trying to do better. He is a sinner by nature and cannot truly change himself. A person has to be born again if he is going to get out of Adam. He has to lose his identity in Adam and get identified with Christ, the last Adam. James Stalker sheds light on man's condition in Adam.

> *From Adam his children derive a sad double heritage — a debt of guilt which they cannot reduce but are constantly increasing, and a carnal nature which is incapable of righteousness. These are the two features of the religious condition of fallen man, and they are the double source of all his woes.*
>
> *But Christ is a new Adam, a new head of humanity, and those who are connected with Him by faith become heirs of a double heritage of a precisely opposite kind. On the one hand, just as through our birth in the first Adam's line we become inevitably entangled in guilt, like a child born into a family which is drowned in debt, so through our birth in the line of the second Adam we get involved in a boundless heritage of merit, which Christ, as the Head of His family, makes the common property of its*

members. *This extinguishes the debt of our guilt and makes us rich in Christ's righteousness. "As by one man's disobedience many were made sinners, so by the obedience of one shall many be made righteous." On the other hand, just as Adam transmitted to his posterity a carnal nature, alien to God and unfit for righteousness, so the new Adam imparts to the race of which He is the Head a spiritual nature, akin to God and delighting in righteousness.*

THE LAW OF SIN

But God be thanked, that ye were the servants of sin, but ye have obeyed from the heart that form of doctrine which was delivered you. Being then made free from sin, you became the servants of righteousness.

- Romans 6:17,18

SIN ALWAYS COSTS MORE THAN YOU WANT TO PAY, TAKES YOU FARTHER THAN YOU WANT TO GO, AND KEEPS YOU LONGER THAN YOU WANT TO STAY.

Paul said that we were once the servants of sin. Sin makes you do things you do not want to do. Sin is breaking the laws of God, breaking the Word of God, and rebelling against God. To get involved in sin is to become a partner with the devil. *The result of sin is death.*

Initially, sin is offered as pleasure and looks so appealing. The devil does not tell you that he is going to steal from you, kill you, and destroy you. He will not tell you that up front. In fact, he likes you to think he does not exist!

The Bible says there is pleasure in sin for a season (Hebrews 11:25). The devil does not tell you that the wages of sin is death, or that it breaks your fellowship with God and causes your destiny to be the same as his. Sin always costs more than you want to pay, takes you farther than you want to go, and keeps you longer than you want to stay. The devil is trying to get as many people to go to hell with him as he can.

> *Now if I do that I would not, it is no more I that do it, but sin that dwelleth in me. I find then a law, that, when I would do good, evil is present with me.*
>
> *- Romans 7:20,21*

Sin is not just something that a person does. Sin is a nature that gets a hold of people, controls their lives, and

destroys them.   *Sin breaks your fellowship with God.*
Everything that God has deposited in you — the potential
and the possibilities — will never be realized as long as sin
controls your life. Your self-esteem and self-image are
rotted out by sin.

SIN IS NOT JUST SOMETHING THAT A PERSON DOES. SIN IS A NATURE THAT GETS A HOLD OF PEOPLE, CONTROLS THEIR LIVES, AND DESTROYS THEM.

But I see another law in my members, warring against the law of my mind, and bringing me into captivity to the law of sin which is in my members. O wretched man that I am! who shall deliver me from the body of this death! I thank God through Jesus Christ our Lord. So then with the mind I myself serve the law of God; but with the flesh the law of sin.

- Romans 7:23-25

Paul is talking about body, soul, and spirit.   Most
Bible scholars agree that in this chapter, Paul described the
struggle of a person who is not born again but wants to do
what is right. He tries to do right, but he just cannot do it.
There is no hope for man's condition without Jesus Christ.

There is no hope for man outside of the blood of Jesus and His death, burial, and resurrection. Only the blood of Jesus and the power of the Gospel can change a person. God does not just deal with wrongdoing, iniquity, or acts of disobedience to His law and His Word. He deals with the root cause of sin and the very nature of sin in us.

Man's condition in Adam demanded a crucifixion and resurrection. We needed much more than just a lesson, we needed life. Jesus came not to give man just a lesson - but to give us life itself (John 10:10). Many religions give lessons but Jesus Christ came to give us life.

> *For if by one man's offense death reigned by one;*
> *much more they which receive abundance of*
> *grace and of the gift of righteousness shall reign*
> *in life by one, Jesus Christ.*
>
> *- Romans 5:17*

FIRST ADAM, LAST ADAM

Adam's disobedience affected everyone that has ever been or ever will be born. How could one man's sin affect the entire human race?

JESUS CAME NOT TO GIVE MAN JUST A LESSON - BUT TO GIVE US LIFE ITSELF!

A few years ago one of the computers in our main office started to have some problems. For several days, technical support tried to resolve the issues with this computer over the phone. Finally, we had to call in a service technician. After about half an hour, the technician told us that the computer had a boot virus. He really could not explain how this computer had caught this particular virus. At the time, this computer was not internet accessible and did not share files with any other computer.

THERE IS NO HOPE FOR MAN'S CONDITION WITHOUT JESUS CHRIST.

No one was extremely concerned because we had back-up files for all of the work done on this computer. The technician began to tell the worker who used this computer that the operating system was corrupt. He said that the only way to fix the computer was to erase the memory.

The worker still did not show much concern; after all, we had back-up files for everything. The technician started to explain that because the operating system was corrupt, all of the back-up files were corrupt also. The back-up files could not be used when the memory was erased and the programs restored. The files also could not be used on any other computer. The corrupted files would corrupt any computer system if they were used. The back-up files had been made in the corrupt operating system and would corrupt the system again. The computer could still be used, but all of the information was lost. The back-up files had to be destroyed.

Mankind, because of Adam's sin, became corrupt. One man, "operating system Adam," infected the entire human race.

THAT FORM OF DOCTRINE

But God be thanked, that ye were the servants of sin, but ye have obeyed from the heart that form of doctrine which was delivered you. Being then made free from sin, ye became the servants of righteousness.

- Romans 6:17,18

People seldom think of doctrine as setting them free from sin. Most people think of some great evangelist waving his hand over them, being slain in the Spirit, and then suddenly, miraculously, they are free from sin! I believe in the power of God, in the moving of the Holy Ghost, and in the anointing. Notice what Paul said, "You obeyed from your heart *a form of doctrine* that was delivered you, and *it set you free from sin.*"

Many people say, "I do not read the Bible, but I have this problem that I need someone to take care of." Paul has the answer in "this form of doctrine." He said it was delivered to you and you were instructed in the system of truth.

As Paul wrote, the Holy Ghost wove a system of truth through all of his letters to keep people in the center of the Gospel and who they are in Christ. In between the historical references he wove timeless, eternal truths.

In Romans 6:17,18 Paul said, "This doctrine will set you free from sin. You will become a servant of righteousness." The dreams, plans, and purposes that God has put in your life will take you where you need to go if you will stay in this form of doctrine.

BREAKING THE POWER OF SIN

If you get to know some of the prisoners in the penitentiaries, you wonder how they could have done what they are accused of doing. Most of them are not so bad. A man or woman who is not born again still has a conscience and, for the most part, wants to do what is right.

ONCE WE ARE BORN AGAIN, WE ARE NO LONGER SLAVES TO SIN.

The new birth extends beyond the conscience of man, which tells him right from wrong. The new birth gives man eternal life and establishes God's "righteous nature" within him. Then, he has the ability to break the power and control of sin and the cycle of sin off his mind and body.

God makes us righteous by breaking the power of sin and the effect of sin in our lives. Righteousness is not just something imputed to us — it is the nature of God. His nature comes into us and gives us the desire and the power to change our behavior (Philippians 2:13).

> *There is therefore now no condemnation to them which are in Christ Jesus, who walk not after the flesh, but after the Spirit. For the law of the Spirit of life in Christ Jesus hath made me free from the law of sin and death.*
>
> *- Romans 8:1,2*

Once we are born again, we are no longer slaves to sin. We become servants of righteousness. Righteousness — right standing with God and being pleasing to Him — becomes the governing power in our lives. We desire to do what righteousness wants us to do, not what the old sin nature wants to do.

SLAVES TO RIGHTEOUSNESS

When sin is exposed for what it is, it does not look so appealing. There is no lasting pleasure in it. Paul made very clear where sin came from, how sin got into us, and

71

how sin affects us. Then Paul told us how God dealt with sin in the death, burial, and resurrection of Christ. He explained how believers become servants of righteousness.

THE POWER OF RIGHTEOUSNESS WILL MAKE YOU FREE FROM SIN.

Throughout the book of Romans, Paul shows how you can be a servant of righteousness and how to yield to righteousness. The power of righteousness will make you free from sin. He shows you how you can be free from the past and from the effects and control of sin.

In 1 Corinthians 6:12 Paul said, "All things are lawful for me...but I will not be brought under the power of any." He was adamant and determined. He said, "I will not allow anything to control me — my flesh, my reasoning, my mind, or my feelings. I keep under my body. I bring it into subjection."

Great exploits come out of the lives of people who are slaves to righteousness. Everyone who is made righteous "in Christ" is accepted by God and pleasing to Him. They have favor with Him. Their faith soars and they believe God can do anything! They know how to receive from God.

F I V E

MAN'S CONDITION IN ADAM
System of Truth — Point Three

Wherefore, as by one man sin entered into the world, and death by sin; and so death passed upon all men, for that all have sinned.

- Romans 5:12

I heard the story of a fireman in California whose hand was so severely burned, his doctors determined they would have to amputate. One of the doctors, however, wanted to try an experimental surgery. He knew that the body has certain regenerative powers. He cut the man's side open and inserted the burned hand for a period of time. To the doctor's amazement, when they removed the fireman's hand from his side, it had begun to heal and grow new skin.

I believe God did a similar surgery with man. When Adam sinned, man's condition looked so bad. It looked like God would have to amputate.

SEPARATION FROM GOD

In his alienation and separation from God, Adam actually became an enemy of God. Sacrifices and ordinances had to be followed for anyone to approach God, even at a distance, because of man's condition in Adam. Specific sacrifices were required to be made when the law was broken. The shedding of blood was always required for the atonement of sins.

In the Old Testament, the high priest went into the Holy of Holies only once a year to make exact sacrifices of blood for himself and for the people. When the priest entered the Holy of Holies, he had bells on his garment and a rope tied around him. The people knew as long as they heard the bells ringing, everything was all right. If the high priest did one thing wrong in the presence of God, he would drop dead. The reason he wore the rope was so they could pull his body out of the Holy of Holies.

THE BIBLE IS PROGRESSIVE REVELATION — THERE IS A CONTINUAL REVELATION OF GOD'S REDEMPTION PLAN.

In 2 Samuel 6:3-7, Uzzah broke the laws of God, and the power in the Ark killed him. Actually, Uzzah just tried to help, but they had broken the law in how to transport the Ark. God was not trying to kill him; God is not in the killing business. If they had transported the Ark according to the law God gave to Moses, Uzzah would have never had to reach out to steady it. In ignorance Uzzah did touch the Ark and dropped dead instantly.

THE MOST ACCURATE PICTURE OF GOD COMES THROUGH THE NEW TESTAMENT.

If you break the laws of electricity, you are going to die. Electricity is not out to kill you, but it will kill you on the spot if you get hold of a live wire because of your ignorance or negligence. The power of God is like electricity. Uzzah broke the laws of God and the power of God in the Ark killed him. This happened because of man's condition in Adam — spiritual death and separation from God.

JOB REVEALS MAN'S CONDITION

The Bible is progressive revelation. From the Old Testament to the New Testament, and from the four gospels all the way through the epistles, there is a continual revelation of God's redemption plan. The Old Testament is inspired by God, but the most accurate picture of God comes through the New Testament.

Man's condition in Adam is also seen in the book of Job. Job gives a revelation of man's experience and condition in this world. Some of the things Job said were not necessarily true. He thought God was the One causing the calamities in his life, but it was the devil.

> *If I wash myself with snow water, and make my hands ever so clean; Yet shalt thou plunge me in the ditch, and mine own clothes shall abhor me. For he is not a man, as I am, that I should answer him, and we should come together in judgment. Neither is there any daysman betwixt us, that might lay his hand upon us both.*
>
> *- Job 9:30-33*

Job had boils all over him and had lost his family and all of his possessions. He said, "I am trying to be right with God, but if I wash myself with snow water and make myself clean, you are going to throw me in a ditch, anyway." Job knew that there was nothing he could do to make himself right with God. No matter what he did, it could never be enough.

In verse 32 Job said, "For he is not a man, as I am...." In other words, *God does not know what I am going through. He does not know what it is like to be a man. How can we communicate?* There are three major revelations from the book of Job: man needs righteousness, man needs a revelation of God, and man needs a mediator and a redeemer.

MANKIND NEEDS A MEDIATOR

Neither is there any daysman betwixt us, that might lay his hand upon us both.

> *- Job 9:33*

Neither is there any umpire....

> *- Moffat*

Neither is there any Mediator....

> *- Rotherham*

Job did not know how to get to God; he needed a mediator. He knew he could not go directly to God. He needed someone who could help him get to God. He said he needed someone who might lay his hand on him and God — someone who knew God but could also represent him.

How then can man be justified with God? Or how can he be clean that is born of a woman? Behold even to the moon, and it shineth not; yea, the stars are not pure in his sight. How much less man, that is a worm?

> *- Job 25:4-6*

Job acknowledged that his problem began at birth. He was born with a sinful nature, which separated him from God. Man was meant to stand in dignity before God, but because of sin, man lost his glory, respect, and dignity. Job said, "I am like a worm." This is every person's condition in Adam before the new birth.

When Adam sinned, the earth was cursed and Adam was cursed. When Adam sinned it affected every man in the entire universe. Job said even the universe knows something is wrong. The entire universe is a mess because of Adam's sin. Paul said something similar in Romans 8:22, **"...the whole creation groaneth and travaileth in pain together until now."** Man is under a curse until he is liberated in Christ.

GOD FOUND A SUBSTITUTE

Yea, his soul draweth near unto the grave, and his life to the destroyers. If there be a messenger with him, an interpreter, one among a thousand, to shew unto man his uprightness. Then he is gracious unto him, and saith, Deliver him from going down to the pit: I have found a ransom. His flesh shall be fresher than a child's: he shall return to the days of his youth: He shall pray unto God, and he will be favourable unto him: and he shall see his face with joy: for he will render unto man his righteousness.

- Job 33:22-26

Job prophesied that God had found a ransom. The *Living Bible* says, "I have found a substitute." Jesus is that substitute! Job is talking about redemption! He is talking about favor and rightstanding with God.

> *Lo, all these things worketh God oftentimes with man, To bring back his soul from the pit, to be enlightened with the light of the living.*
>
> *- Job 33:29-30*

In other words, the fire has gone out of man. Yet, God would send the mediator and pay the ransom through the substitutionary work of Christ. He would restore righteousness and set man's spirit on fire again!

Job asked that his words be printed in a book never to be erased (Job 19:23,24). God thought it was a good idea! Under the inspiration of the Holy Spirit, Job saw a larger picture and prophesied: "For I know that my redeemer liveth, and that he shall stand at the latter day upon the earth" (Job 19:25).

PAUL REVEALS MAN'S CONDITION

In the book of Romans, which is primarily about righteousness, Paul describes man's condition.

> *What then? are we better than they? No, in no wise: for we have before proved both Jews and Gentiles, that they are all under sin. As it is*

79

> *written, there is none righteous, no not one: There is none that understandeth, there is none that seeketh after God.*
>
> *- Romans 3:9-10*

> *They are all under the domination of sin, held down by sin and subject to the power and the control of sin.*
>
> *- Romans 3:9,10 - Carpenter's*

Paul said that the Jews have a covenant with God, but they are still controlled by sin. Gentiles have no covenant with God and are also controlled by sin. God had to deal with sin through Christ to break the power of sin for Jews and Gentiles.

> *There is not one who is really wise....*
>
> *- Romans 3:11 - Weymouth*

Paul said that even all the great schools of learning and philosophers of his day in Athens, Corinth, Ephesus, and Alexandria were ignorant and devoid of understanding. Man with all of his knowledge is still alienated from God. When man dies he will go to hell and spend eternity separated from the loving God who created him. This is man's condition in Adam before regeneration in Christ.

WITHOUT HOPE, WITHOUT COVENANT, WITHOUT GOD

Wherefore remember, that ye being in time past Gentiles in the flesh, who are called Uncircumcision by that which is called the Circumcision in the flesh made by hands; That at that time ye were without Christ, being aliens from the commonwealth of Israel, and strangers from the covenants of promise, having no hope, and without God in the world.

- Ephesians 2:11-12

Paul explains your adamic condition before you are born again in Christ. You are without hope, without the covenant, and without God. Your condition in Adam is dead in trespasses and sins. You are not physically or mentally dead, but you are spiritually dead.

He that hath the Son hath life; and he that hath not the Son of God hath not life.

- 1 John 5:12

As I mentioned in the previous chapter, man's condition in Adam demanded a crucifixion and resurrection. We needed much more than just a lesson, we needed life. Jesus came not to give man just a lesson - but to give us

81

life itself (John 10:10). Many religions give lessons but Jesus Christ came to give us life.

MANY RELIGIONS GIVE LESSONS BUT JESUS CHRIST CAME TO GIVE US LIFE.

You can have religion and still be dead. You can serve on the city council and still be dead. You can live in a big, fancy house in the suburbs and still be dead. You can have a store at the mall and still be dead. You can slam-dunk a basketball and still be dead. You can have a tan in Wisconsin and still be dead. You can have your picture on the cover of Time magazine and still be dead. You can even be a priest and wear a robe and still be dead.

SPIRITUALLY DEAD

Wherein in time past ye walked according to the course of this world, according to the prince of the power of the air, the spirit that now worketh in the children of disobedience.

- Ephesians 2:2

You were spiritually dead, through your sins and failures, all the time that you followed this world's ideas of living, and obeyed the evil ruler of the spiritual realm — who is indeed fully operative today in those who disobey God.

- Ephesians 2:1,2 - Phillips

You also has God given life from the dead, for dead you were. Slain by your trespasses and sins in an atmosphere which you had once passed your lives, following the tendency of the present age, controlled by the ruler of the kingdom of the lower air, the demon spirit which is now so active in the children of disobedience.

- Arthur S. Way

Your former lifestyle was controlled by a set of values inspired by the devil.

- Ephesians 2:2, Johnson

When you are spiritually dead you follow the course of this world. When you follow the course of this world, the prince of the power of the air —the spirit that works in the children of disobedience — controls you.

Paul is talking about a spiritual condition that was passed on to you from Adam that allows the devil to dominate you. If you are living with the world's standards as a measure for what is right and wrong, you are obeying its unseen ruler, the devil. The course of this world will take you straight to hell.

CONTROLLED BY THE DEVIL

If your values and philosophy of life make no room for eternity and you do not see that you will one day stand before God, you are being deceived. When you live only in the light of the present and what makes you happy now, you are living under the devil's influence. You are being controlled by the devil.

> *You drifted along with the tide. You were not a master of your own fate, and you are not a captain of your own soul. The windy gust of passion and self-will, the devilish promptings of the evil one threw you this way and then threw you that way....*
>
> *- Ephesians 2:2,3 - Carpenter*

> *You are ridden by the passions of your sensual nature, obeying the impulses of that nature and its dark imaginings of your mind.*
>
> *- Arthur S. Way*

> *...obeying the orders of our bodies and of our imaginations.*
>
> *- Noli*

> *Among whom also we all had our conversation [lifestyle] in times past in the lusts of our flesh,*

fulfilling the desires of the flesh and of the mind; and were by nature the children of wrath.

- Ephesians 2:3

Paul says you are following the course of this world, thinking you are the captain of your soul. When in reality, you are controlled by the devil and you don't even know it. Your condition has subjected you to the wrath of God. When you follow the lust of your flesh and of your mind, you are opening yourself up to the wrath of God.

IN ADAM - IN CHRIST

Therefore by the deeds of the law there shall no flesh be justified in his sight: for by the law is the knowledge of sin. For all have sinned, and come short of the glory of God; Being justified freely by his grace through the redemption that is in Christ Jesus: Whom God hath set forth to be a propitiation through faith in his blood, to declare his righteousness for the remission of sins that are past, through the forbearance of God. To declare, I say, at this time his righteousness: that he might be just, and the justifier of him which believeth in Jesus.

- Romans 3:20,23-26

85

Understanding man's condition in Adam helps us see the necessity of the cross of Christ. In his letters, Paul went into great detail describing man's condition in Adam to show us the extent of our salvation in Christ. Not only does Paul describe man's standing before God, but he also describes how the flesh and the mind control unregenerated man.

> *All of us were bound in that state at one time; responding only to the satanically inspired impulses of our evil natures so that we too were led to obey the cravings of our instincts and went about satisfying the longings of our flesh. Like others, we did not realize we were accumulating God's wrath and that our very natures were sending us to hell.*
>
> *- Ephesians 2:3, Lovett's*

He contrasts our condition in Adam with our position in Christ like a jewelry store displays its diamonds against a background of black velvet. Paul paints the picture of man's background so we can see it like the cut of a diamond and every facet of what God has done for us in Christ. We see the wisdom, love, purity, righteousness, and power of God on display on the dark background of man's sinful condition.

> *But God, who is rich in mercy, for his great love*
> *wherewith he loved us, Even when we were dead*
> *in sins, hath quickened us together with Christ,*
> *(by grace ye are saved;) And hath raised us up*
> *together, and made us sit together in heavenly*
> *places in Christ Jesus: That in the ages to come*
> *he might shew the exceeding riches of his grace*
> *in his kindness toward us through Christ Jesus.*
>
> *- Ephesians 2:4-7*

The word "quickened" means *He has given us life —*
spiritual life. This life restores dominion to the point that we
are no longer controlled by our flesh or our minds. We are
not dominated by the devil. We are not following the course
of this world any longer. *We are quickened together with*
Christ.

Paul told us to be thankful to God for all things:
thankful for giving us the victory; thankful for always
causing us to triumph; thankful for qualifying us for our
inheritance in Christ; thankful for delivering us from the
power of darkness and for translating us into the kingdom
of His dear Son. In Christ, you have redemption through
His blood, even the forgiveness of sin.

Everything we need pertaining to life and godliness
has been provided in Christ (2 Peter 1:3). What is left to
do? Study the Word and find out who you are in Christ.

Acknowledge and declare, "I am who God says I am. I am a new creation in Christ. Old things have passed away. Everything has become new. I was identified with Christ in His death, burial, and resurrection, and now I am in union with Him. I am no longer in Adam — I am in Christ!"

SIX

WHAT HAPPENED TO JESUS FROM THE CROSS TO THE THRONE

System of Truth — Point Four

ONCE UPON A TIME

Everyone likes a great story that begins with the phrase, "Once upon a time...." The story of Jesus is the greatest story ever told. It is not a fantasy, but a true story that has changed the world for thousands of years. The story of Jesus is told in over a thousand languages to millions of people, young and old, around the world and is still changing lives today! One day as I was studying Hebrews chapters 9 and 10, the word "ONCE" stood out so clearly. I began to see God's plan of redemption in Christ and how the wisdom and power of God very effectively "ONCE" paid the price for our freedom.

> *Neither by the blood of goats and calves, but by*
> *his own blood he entered in ONCE into the holy*
> *place, having obtained eternal redemption for us.*
> *- Hebrews 9:12*

> *He went ONCE for all into the [Holy of] Holies...*
> *but with His own blood, having found and*
> *secured a complete redemption (an everlasting*
> *release for us).*
>
> *- Amplified*

Whenever you face any challenge, remember this story and tell it again -- Once Upon a Time! When Satan comes against you, just bring up this story and say, "once upon a time..." and the devil will leave. Now, we as believers can take the Word of God and tell the devil a bedtime story. Say, "Devil, ONCE upon a time Jesus defeated you for all eternity." Speak the Word of God with boldness and rock the devil to sleep!

> *In whom we have redemption through his blood,*
> *even the forgiveness of sins, according to the*
> *riches of his grace.*
>
> *- Ephesians 1:7*

From the cross to the throne, Jesus paid for our redemption, deliverance, freedom, and healing. Paul continually emphasized that Jesus purchased our redemption to make us free from sin. "Redemption" simply means "freedom or deliverance through the payment of a price." Again and again Paul tells us that Jesus obtained eternal redemption for us *through His blood.*

*In whom we have redemption through his blood,
even the forgiveness of sins.*

- Colossians 1:14

THE FOUR MAJOR VIEWS OF THE ATONEMENT

Much was taking place in the death, burial and resurrection of Jesus Christ, more than what meets the natural eye of a casual reader. It was a production of God and is the central focal point of history and the plan of redemption. These are four major views of what happened in these events and how they affect us today.

1. SUBSTITUTION OR SATISFACTION: Jesus took man's place, died his death and became sin for every man. In becoming a substitute for sinful man, He satisfied the demands of a holy God. He took our place on the cross and identified with us in our sin, sickness and sorrow so that they could be removed. He was buried, justified, triumphed over evil, and raised to sit at the right hand of God.

*Surely he hath borne our griefs and carried our
sorrows: yet we did esteem him stricken, smitten
of God and afflicted. But he was wounded for
our transgressions, he was bruised for our*

91

iniquities: the chastisement of our peace was upon him; and with his stripes we are healed. All we like sheep have gone astray; we have turned every one to his own way; and the Lord hath laid on him the iniquity of us all.

- Isaiah 53:4-6

He shall see the travail of his soul, and shall be satisfied: by his knowledge shall my righteous servant justify many; for he shall bear their iniquities.

- Isaiah 53:11

When he sees all that is accomplished by his anguish, he will be satisfied. And because of his experience, my righteous servant will make it possible for many to be counted righteous, for he will bear their sins.

- Isaiah 53:11 TLB

Who was delivered for our offenses, and was raised again for our justification.

- Romans 4:25

Who was delivered up because of our offenses, and was raised up because of our being declared righteous.

- Romans 4:25 Young

For he hath made him to be sin for us, who knew
no sin; that we might be made the righteousness
of God in him.

- 2 Corinthians 5:21

Him, who had no acquaintance with sin, God, for
our sakes, treated as an embodiment of Sin, in
order that we, in our part, might become,
through union with Him, an embodiment of the
righteousness that God desires.

- Wade

2. THE RANSOM VIEW: Man was held hostage by the lord of death and Jesus became the ransom in order to redeem us back to God. By His obedience, Jesus overthrew the kingdom of darkness and took back the authority Adam had lost through disobedience. We see Jesus is Lord. He is Victor!

Forasmuch then as the children are partakers of
flesh and blood, he also himself likewise took
part of the same; that through death he might
destroy him that had the power of death, that is
the devil; and deliver them, who through fear of
death were all their lifetime subject to bondage.

- Hebrews 2:14,15

...He might put an end to Him who possesseth the lordship of death...

> *- Weekes*

And having spoiled principalities and powers, he made a show of them openly, triumphing over them in it.

> *- Colossians 2:15*

He set Himself and us free from all the spirit powers of evil...

> *- Deane*

And the hostile princes and rulers He shook off from Himself, and boldly displayed them as His conquests...

> *- Weymouth*

I am he that liveth, and was dead; and, behold, I am alive forevermore, Amen; and have the keys of hell and of death.

> *- Revelation 1:18*

3. THE BLOOD COVENANT: Through the offering of His own blood Jesus became a perfect sacrifice. He once for all, by the shedding of His blood and His death, fulfilled the Old Covenant and activated the New Covenant based on better promises. For more complete study on the blood of Jesus, see our book, *The Bloodline of a Champion.*

Whom God put forward (before the eyes of all) as a mercy seat and propitiation by His blood (the cleansing and life-giving sacrifice of atonement and reconciliation, to be received) through faith. This was to show God's righteousness, because in His divine forbearance He had passed over and ignored former sins without punishment.

- Romans 3:25 (Amplified)

Now the God of peace, that brought again from the dead our Lord Jesus, that great shepherd of the sheep, through the blood of the everlasting covenant, make you perfect in every good work....

- Hebrews 13:20, 21

4. THE MORAL VIEW OR THE LOVE OF GOD: The driving force behind the death, burial and resurrection is God's great love for mankind.

For God commended His love toward us, in that, while we were yet sinners, Christ died for us.

- Romans 5:8

Yet the proof of God's amazing love is this....

- Phillips

JESUS TOOK UPON HIMSELF OUR CURSE

> *Christ hath redeemed us from the curse of the*
> *law, being made a curse for us: for it is written,*
> *Cursed is every one that hangeth on a tree.*
>
> *- Galatians 3:13*

Jesus did not die the death of a martyr; He died as our substitute. It was important that Jesus die the death on the cross to fulfill the law concerning our redemption from the penalty of sin. Jesus knew the price, the penalty for sin, and knew He would pay that penalty. He knew that for a moment in time He would be made sin, be made a curse, be separated from His Father, and descend into the heart of the earth.

Other religions do not see the necessity of the crucifixion of Jesus because they do not understand man's condition. Many religions offer us many lessons, but Jesus Christ gives more than a lesson - He gives us life itself. Jesus did not just die for you. An exchange took place. He was made a curse so you might be redeemed from the curse of the law. What happened in Jesus' death and resurrection was far greater than everything He did while He was on earth. In His earthly ministry He dealt with the "branch offices" of evil. In His death and resurrection, He went to the headquarters of evil and took care of evil for every person for all time.

96

JESUS CAME TO DIE

When the time came for Jesus to go to the cross, He said, "To this end was I born..." (John 18:37). Jesus is "...the Lamb slain from the foundation of the world" (Revelation 13:8). Jesus was not afraid of physical death; he was no coward — Jesus came to die.

> *...I lay down my life, that I might take it again. No man taketh it from me, but I lay it down of myself. I have power to lay it down, and I have power to take it again.*
>
> *- John 10:17,18*

> *Thinkest thou that I cannot pray to my Father, and he shall presently give me more than twelve legions of angels? But how then shall the scriptures be fulfilled, that thus it must be?*
>
> *- Matthew 26:53,54*

IN THE GARDEN OF GETHSEMANE

Jesus slept in the middle of a storm, walked on the water, raised the dead, cast out devils, and healed every kind of sickness and infirmity. In every situation, He was the Master. When the time came to go to the cross, He entered a state of shock, grief, and distress so severe that He could hardly function.

97

Then cometh Jesus with them unto a place called Gethsemane, and saith unto the disciples, Sit ye here, while I go pray yonder. And he took with him Peter and the two sons of Zebedee, and began to be sorrowful and very heavy. Then saith he unto them, My soul is exceeding sorrowful, even unto death: tarry ye here, and watch with me. And he went a little further, and fell on his face, and prayed, saying, O my Father, if it be possible, let this cup pass from me: nevertheless not as I will, but as thou wilt. And he cometh unto the disciples, and findeth them asleep, and saith unto Peter, What, could ye not watch with me one hour? Watch and pray, that ye enter not into temptation: the spirit indeed is willing, but the flesh is weak. He went away again the second time, and prayed, saying, O my Father, if this cup may not pass away from me, except I drink it, thy will be done. And he came and found them asleep again: for their eyes were heavy.

- Matthew 26:36-43

Luke 22:43 says that Jesus was so full of grief that an angel had to come and strengthen Him lest He die prematurely. Sorrow and grief came upon Jesus in

98

Gethsemane because He was about to be made a curse for us, the substitute who would die our death. The disciples had never seen Jesus like this. The *Good News Bible* says, "He began to show grief and distress of mind." One translation of Matthew 26:37 says, "In the anguish and the desolation that came upon Him now...."

> *He began to be distressed and overwhelmed. He then said, My soul is very full of grief, even to death.*
>
> *- Matthew 26:37,38 - Fenton*

> *My soul is crushed with horror and sadness to the point of death...stay here...stay awake with me.*
>
> *- The Living Bible*

Jesus pleaded with his disciples, "Please stay awake, please pray with me, please help me out." Jesus literally went into shock.

> *Horror and dismay came over Him.*
>
> *- Mark 14:33 - New English*

> *...and [He] began to be full of terror and distress, and he said to them, My heart is oppressed with anguish to the very point of death....*
>
> *- Mark 14:33,34 - Weymouth*

And [He] began to be horror-stricken and desperately depressed.

- Phillips

The increasing realization of what lay ahead came to Him with such a sense of overwhelming shock, that He was distraught in His mind. He said, My soul is grief-stricken with a grief like unto death.

- Barclay

SEPARATION FROM THE FATHER

If Jesus were to die the death of a martyr, He would only be dying His own death. However, He was facing the death of a sinner. He was taking our condition — the death we deserve. What Jesus went through on the cross cannot be adequately described. He had always been with the Father. Now for a moment in time, He was going to become sin for us and be completely separated from the Father.

Abba, Father, all things are possible unto thee; take away this cup from me: nevertheless not what I will, but what thou wilt.

- Mark 14:36

Jesus said, "God, if there is any other way that man can be redeemed without Me being made sin and going to the cross — being separated from you — let it happen. If there is not another way, not My will, but Your will be done."

Imagine a person who had lived holy and righteous in the presence of God their entire life. How repulsed they would be when subjected by force to some filthy act of sin! Jesus is the only person who ever walked the earth to never know sin. Yet, He Who knew no sin became sin for us (2 Corinthians 5:21)! Jesus became our substitute, willingly taking upon Himself the wrath of the Father for our sins, truly tasting death for all men and receiving our just punishment.

THE CUP OF GOD'S WRATH

In his book *The Cross and the New Testament*, Leon Morris says:

> *It was not death as such that He feared, it*
> *was the particular death that He was to die —*
> *that death in which He was one with sinners,*
> *sharing their lot, bearing their sins, dying their*
> *death. Nor should we overlook His reference*

*to the drinking of the cup. This is usually
taken as no more than a metaphor for
suffering.*

C.E. Cranfield points out that in the Old Testament
the metaphorical use of cup refers predominately to God's
punishment of human sin. He concludes that this cup is
God's wrath against sin.

When Jesus said, "Let this cup pass from me"
(Matthew 26:39), He knew that the cup of God's wrath and
anger against sin was now filled and He was to drink it until
it was totally empty. Jesus took God's wrath against you
and me and against sin. He became our substitute so we
could be right with God, be pleasing to Him, and accepted
before Him.

On the cross, Jesus became our substitute for the
penalty of sin. He was made a curse for us. He took the
punishment we deserve and that a holy God demands. He
took the wrath of God that was against us so we could be
welcomed into God's presence approved and forgiven.
Christ redeemed us from the curse of the law.

ENGRAFTED INTO CHRIST

*Therefore if any person is [engrafted] in Christ
(the Messiah) he is a new creation (a new*

creature altogether); the old [previous moral and spiritual condition] has passed away. Behold, the fresh and new has come!

- 2 Corinthians 5:17 - Amplified

I live in an area where there are a lot of plant nurseries. These nurseries grow millions and millions of plants that are shipped all over the United States. One thing I have learned from the nurseries is the engrafting process.

When you want to engraft a plant you must make a cut on the plant. In order for the branch to grow into the plant correctly you must make an identical cut on the branch. Then, you must put that branch inside of the open wound of the plant and wrap them together and they become one. There is no grafting without wounding.

Surely he hath borne our griefs, and carried our sorrows: yet we did esteem him stricken, smitten of God, and afflicted. But he was <u>wounded</u> for our transgressions, he was bruised for our iniquities: the chastisement of our peace was upon him; and with his stripes we are healed.

- Isaiah 53:4-5

103

What happened when He was wounded? He was wounded with the identical condition that we had. We were put right into Him, and our condition was engrafted into Christ.

JESUS — FIRST BORN FROM THE DEAD

I am he that liveth, and was dead; and, behold, I am alive for evermore. Amen; and have the keys of hell and of death.

- Revelation 1:18

Jesus tasted death for every man in his death and resurrection. One translation says that He was the first man to enter the death experience and master it. Jesus entered the death experience when He was made to be sin for us. Satan thought he had the Son of God, but God declared Him righteous and quickened Him by the Spirit (1 Peter 3:18). He was made alive, and we are made alive with Him (Ephesians 2:1).

JESUS WAS WOUNDED WITH THE IDENTICAL CONDITION THAT WE HAD. WE WERE PUT RIGHT INTO HIM, AND OUR CONDITION WAS ENGRAFTED INTO CHRIST.

God's voice rang out with a declaration of righteousness from Heaven, "Thou art my Son, this day have I begotten thee" (Acts 13:33). God's voice reverberated all the way down into the heart of the earth, and hell began to shake. Demons trembled and ran in total confusion and utter defeat.

> *And having spoiled principalities and powers, he made a shew of them openly, triumphing over them in it.*
>
> *- Colossians 2:15*

When God declared Jesus righteous, He was born again. The Bible says Jesus is the firstborn from the dead (Romans 8:29). Jesus was the first man ever to be born again.

SATAN'S MASTERY DESTROYED

When you understand man's condition and what happened to Jesus from the cross to the throne, you will say, "I was there. His crucifixion was my crucifixion. His death was my death. His curse was my curse. His shame was my shame. His separation from God was my separation from God. His burial was my burial. I was buried with Him. His descent into the heart of the earth was my descent into the heart of the earth. His sufferings were my sufferings."

Paul saw that in the resurrection, Christ destroyed Satan's mastery over the human race forever. Jesus did not just cast out a legion of demons in Capernaum. He went into hell's home office and dethroned the devil for all eternity!

Jesus destroyed the devil, put him to naught, and paralyzed him. The devil has never been, nor will he ever be the same again!

> *That through death he might destroy him that had the power of death, that is the devil.*
>
> *- Hebrews 2:14*

> *Blotting out the handwriting of ordinances that was against us, which was contrary to us, and took it out of the way, nailing it to his cross; And having spoiled principalities and powers, he made a shew of them openly, triumphing over them in it.*
>
> *- Colossians 2:14,15*

In Ephesians 1:19,20 Paul said, "I am praying that you will be able to see the exceeding greatness of God's power to us who believe, according to the working of His mighty power which He wrought in Christ when He raised Him from the dead."

The resurrection of Jesus Christ is the greatest display of power in the history of the universe. The reason such tremendous power was used was because Jesus was destroying everything Satan did in Adam and He was making a new creation. This power is available to every believer.

THE RESURRECTION OF JESUS CHRIST IS THE GREATEST DISPLAY OF POWER IN THE HISTORY OF THE UNIVERSE.

When you fully understand what happened to Jesus from the cross to the throne, you will hold your head up high! You will say, "Devil, you better take your hands off me. Jesus paid the price for me, and I refuse to be bound. Take your hands off my mind, my body, my family, and my finances. You have no right to touch or interfere with any aspect of my life!"

SEVEN

YOUR IDENTIFICATION WITH CHRIST
System of Truth — Point Five

JESUS IN YOUR JERSEY

He that spared not his own Son, but delivered him up for us all, how shall he not with him also freely give us all things?

- Romans 8:32

How, then, shall we respond to all this? If God is rootin' for us, who can win over us? If he didn't hold back his own Son, but put Him in the game for us all, won't He even more gladly, in addition to his Son, equip us with all we need to win the game?

- Jordan

I played football in high school so I know what it means to come in the game for somebody. If you have ever watched a football game on TV, you hear announcers giving their commentary on what is taking place in the game. You may hear the announcer talk about a particular player, let's say number 65 (that was my number in high school). The guys on the other team are whipping him all over the field, stomping him really bad, he is bleeding, and has grass stains and dirt all over him. Every time the ball is hiked number 65 gets slaughtered. He gets pushed so far back that you think he's on the other team. Number 65 is just being dominated by the other team. Then the coach says, "I've got a plan." He pulls number 65 out and replaces him with the strongest man on the team.

GOD MOVED ON THE INSIDE OF YOU AND GOT IN YOUR JERSEY, HE IDENTIFIED WITH YOU SO YOU COULD IDENTIFY WITH HIM.

That's what God did for us when He sent Jesus to die in our place. God put Jesus in number 65's (mankind's) jersey. Number 65 runs back on the field, and now the whole picture changes. The announcer says, "You know something has happened to number 65. He's kicking that ball all over the field now."

Before man was identified with Christ (in His death, burial, and resurrection) depression, discouragement, fear, failure, shame, and guilt had whipped him all over. But now, number 65 is winning and now he's dominating. What happened was God saw man's condition and knew that he could not train you enough to change the game. He knew He is going to have to get in your jersey. There's no other way. He said, "We can't train them, let's just jump on the inside of them and I'll live on the inside of them, I'll walk in them." The incarnation is when God got in your jersey. You say, "Yeah, but that's Jesus." When you were born again there was another incarnation. God moved on the inside of you and got in your jersey, He identified with you so you could identify with Him.

> *I am crucified with Christ: nevertheless I live; yet not I, but Christ liveth in me: and the life which I now live in the flesh I live by the faith of the Son of God, who loved me, and gave himself for me.*
>
> *- Galatians 2:20*

GOD IS IN THE BUSINESS OF CHANGING IDENTITIES.

Identification is defined in *Webster's Dictionary* as: "to consider or treat as the same, the condition or fact of being, the same in all qualities under consideration." These words are all related to each other: identification, identity, identical, and identified. Many people live and die and never really find their true identity.

EVERYTHING THAT SATAN DID IN ADAM, GOD REVERSED IN CHRIST.

Have you ever checked in for a flight and been asked for proof of identification? You can say, "Here I am. Can't you see - this is me? I can prove that I exist. Just look." Even when I played baseball in elementary school, they wanted to see my birth certificate! I could have said, "Look, I can prove I was born. Here I am." That was not enough; I needed some authentic, legal, official proof that I was who I said I was. This is all a part of life in this natural world.

In the realm of the Spirit you say, "Well, here I am. Obviously, I am who I am." God will ask, "Do you have any identification on you?" You say, "I sure do, I have some identification right here in Galatians 2:20: 'I am crucified with Christ: nevertheless I live; yet not I but Christ liveth in me....' That is my identification with Christ. I am with Him."

ONE WITH THE MASTER

A.J. Gordon said, "For every statement made about Christ in His death and resurrection, there is a *parallel* statement made about the believer, so that Christ and the believer are one together." It is true that parallel statements can be made but there really is no parallel because parallels never meet! A.J. Gordon went on to say, "The glory and the mystery of the believer's life is that he or she is one with the Master — inseparable from Him. It is not a life running alongside his, and taking shape and direction from it. It is his life reenacted in his followers; the reproduction in them of those events which are immoral in energy and limitless in application." That is your identification with Christ. 1 Corinthians 6:17 says, "But he that is joined unto the Lord is one spirit." You are one with Christ and *in Christ.* Your spirit is joined with His Spirit.

CRUCIFIED TOGETHER WITH CHRIST

> *Knowing this, that our old man is crucified with him, that the body of sin might be destroyed, that henceforth we should not serve sin. For he that is dead is freed from sin.*
>
> *- Romans 6:6, 7*

> *The old person we used to be was nailed to the cross with Him....*
>
> *- Cressman*

> *...our old inherited self was crucified with Him....*
>
> *- Bruce*

> *...our former evil identities have been executed,*
> *so to speak.*
>
> *- Richert*

Jesus died on the cross, but Paul said something else happened on the cross. Your old man or the "old person" you used to be before you were born again, was crucified with Him.

The "old man" (as we have seen in point three) also represents the old man that was in Adam, the race that Adam produced, and the condition passed on to us from our first birth in Adam. Paul said that anything produced by Adam was crucified with Christ. Everything that Satan did in Adam, God reversed in Christ.

If you have been crucified with Christ, then you are also dead and therefore free from sin. Romans 6:11 says, "...reckon ye also yourselves to be dead indeed unto sin...." The word "reckon" is an accounting term which simply means "to consider" or "account it to be so."

> *Let us consider ourselves as actually dead to*
> *sin.*
>
> *- New Berkely*

> *You no less can count yourselves dead so far as*
> *sin is concerned.*
>
> *- Authentic*

DEAD TO THIS WORLD

I am crucified with Christ: nevertheless I live; yet not I, but Christ liveth in me: and the life which I now live in the flesh I live by the faith of the Son of God, who loved me, and gave himself for me.

- Galatians 2:20

With Christ I have been co-crucified.

- Marshall

Christ took me to the cross with Him.

- Laubach

You also are to account yourselves to be in relation to sin, dead men.

- Way

What did Paul mean when he said, I have been crucified with Christ? This throws theologians off. They ask how Paul could say he was crucified with Christ when Jesus was crucified with two thieves. Paul was not even in Jerusalem at the time, but Paul was not speaking from a natural standpoint.

Our old man is crucified with him.

- Romans 6:6

115

> *But God forbid that I should glory, save in the cross of our Lord Jesus Christ, by whom the world is crucified unto me, and I unto the world.*
>
> *- Galatians 6:14*

> *For in Christ Jesus neither circumcision availeth any thing, nor uncircumcision, but a new creature.*
>
> *- Galatians 6:15*

> *[The world] has no more influence on me, than if it were not.*
>
> *- Locke*

Satan is the god of this world. Many people are influenced by this world and the spirits of this world. They are influenced by the lust of the eyes, the lust of the flesh, and the pride of life. They are controlled by fame, prestige, and money. They are trying to be somebody in this world. Paul said, "I died to this world."

ALIVE UNTO GOD

> *I consider myself as having died and now enjoying a second existence, which is simply Jesus using my body.*
>
> *- Galatians 2:20 - Distilled Bible*

116

This gives us a little different picture of Christianity than what is generally seen today. You can say that Jesus is with you, you are following Him, and Jesus has saved you. When you come across Paul's letter he says, "I am crucified with Christ, and I am not even alive anymore. Christ lives inside of me. It is Jesus using my body. You see me, but it's really not me. The old Paul [Saul] died. Everything about him died — his ambitions and desires. He was crucified with Christ. He is dead and gone. All that is left now is Jesus."

Paul also said, "For me to live is Christ" (Philippians 1:21). He is not only saying to reckon ourselves to be dead unto sin, but also to see ourselves as "...alive unto God through Jesus Christ our Lord" (Romans 6:11).

You were not only crucified with Christ, but you died with Christ. You not only died with Christ, but you were buried with Him. You were not only buried with Christ, but you were quickened and made alive in Him. You were not only made alive with Christ, but you were raised with Him. You were not only raised with Christ, but you are seated together with Him. You are not only seated with Christ, but you share the authority of His resurrection and His power. You share the authority of His throne. You are triumphant in Him. We are not going to stay at the cross. We are

117

going from the cross to the throne. Many people want to go to the throne, but you have to go to the cross first, then on to the throne.

JOINT-HEIRS WITH CHRIST

You are not just seated with Christ, you are blessed *with Him.* Paul says we are heirs of God and *joint-heirs* with Jesus Christ. This is your identification with Christ. God is in the business of changing identities.

> *I have been crucified with Christ. Now it is not my old self, but Christ Himself, who lives in me.*
> *- Galatians 2:20 - Noli*

You should be doing pretty good if Christ Himself lives in you! Jesus is triumphant. He is the Master. He is the Boss. He has conquered the devil, the world, and the flesh.

JOINT HEIR - EQUAL POSSESSION BECAUSE OF EQUAL POSITION.

You can look at this as theology or as a reality. If you think too much about it, you will never figure it out. If you just accept it at face value and say, "That is what Paul said, and that is God's revelation of Christianity to me. That is what I am, and that is what I have," then you won't get into a lot of theology and mental reasoning trying to figure it out.

> *I have been crucified with Christ and, I live now not with my own life but with the life of Christ who lives in me. The life I now live in this body, I live in faith — faith in the Son of God who loved me and sacrificed Himself for my sake.*
>
> *- Galatians 2:20 - Jerusalem Bible*

Someone said to me, "Pastor, in all the sermons we have heard about what happened on the cross, the preacher always identified us with the crowd — the Roman soldiers, Mary the mother of Jesus, the disciples, or someone else in the crowd who was hollering, 'Crucify Him!' No one ever told us that we were identified with Christ." Paul did not identify with the crowd, he identified with Christ. He said, "I was crucified with Christ, and there I died with Him."

I IDENTIFIED MYSELF COMPLETELY WITH HIM. INDEED, I HAVE BEEN CRUCIFIED WITH CHRIST. MY EGO IS NO LONGER CENTRAL. IT IS NO LONGER IMPORTANT THAT I APPEAR RIGHTEOUS BEFORE YOU OR HAVE YOUR GOOD OPINION, AND I AM NO LONGER DRIVEN TO IMPRESS GOD. CHRIST LIVES IN ME.
- GALATIANS 2:20 (MESSAGE)

JESUS DEFEATED THE DEVIL

The devil still can't figure it all out! He knew God had a plan to redeem man, he just didn't know how it was going to happen. The Bible says that if he would have known, he never would have crucified the Lord of Glory (1 Corinthians 2:8).

When he stung the Son of God with death, he was like a bee that loses its stinger and then goes off and dies. Jesus took the sting of death for every person. He dethroned the devil who had the power of death.

The devil is saying, "How can this be?" This is a legal covenant that God made with man. This covenant is legal because of the incarnation. When Jesus came to earth and put on flesh by being born of a woman, He legally became our substitute. He became the second Adam (Romans 5:14). This was the plan from the beginning. Back in the Garden, God revealed how it would all happen. In Genesis 3:15, He said that the seed of woman (Jesus) would bruise the serpent's (Satan's) head.

Paul said that one man, Jesus Christ, died for every man. Since He died for every man, then every man died in Him. How is it possible that one man could die for every man?

For the love of Christ constraineth us; because we thus judge, that if one died for all, then were all dead.

- 2 Corintians 5:14

...now that we recognize that one man died for everyone, which means that they all share in his death.

- Good News Bible

We know that Christ died for all of us. So our old self died with Him.

- Laubach

Jesus did not come to prove He could conquer the devil. That would be no match! Jesus became a man so the victory He accomplished would be for all mankind. Jesus won the victory in the confines of human life. So Jesus' victory was not just for the Godhead, but also for all of mankind.

A NEW IDENTITY IN CHRIST

Understanding your identification with Christ is the center of the Gospel. Paul had such a radical identity change that he said, "It is not even me living anymore."

121

That is a radical identity change! Someone said that the power of God hit Paul so hard on the road to Damascus that it knocked the "S" off the front of his name and replaced it with a "P." He was never Saul again!

If you committed a crime, the prosecution could grant you immunity from prosecution in exchange for your testimony against the Mafia. The FBI might promise you a new identity. They would change all of your records — your fingerprints, your address, and your social security number. They would move you to a new location and change every record concerning every bill that you owe. They would totally wipe out your past and give you a new identity.

How does God change your identity? The moment you receive Christ, you become a new creation in Him. It may take you a while before you can say, "I'm not even that person anymore!" However, as you feed on the Word of God, it will become real to you.

The devil may have been after you for years, but God has wiped out all record of your past — every account that was against you — every sin, every claim the devil had on you! "As far as the east is from the west, so far hath he removed our transgressions from us" (Psalm 103:12).

God has changed your old address and now you live "in Christ." If you stay where He has relocated you, the devil cannot find you! Do not talk about your feelings or past failures. Do not give the devil another shot at you. "For ye are dead, and your life is hid with Christ in God" (Colossians 3:3). God says, "Your old nature passed away. You have a new identity now!"

FIND YOUR IDENTITY IN THE WORD

When John the Baptist came out of the wilderness preaching, people asked him, "Who are you?" They asked if he was the prophet Elijah come back (John 1:19-22). John simply quoted from Isaiah 40:3. He answered, "I am the voice of one crying in the wilderness, Make straight the way of the Lord..." (John 1:23). In other words, he opened his Bible and said, "Let me tell you who I am. It is written right here." This is the key to your identification with Christ — *finding out who the Word says you are.*

EVEN JESUS FOUND HIMSELF IN THE SCRIPTURES.

As a teenager I struggled with my own identity. The Lord showed me that even Jesus had to find Himself in the Word. Even though Jesus was deity, He had to lay aside His deity power when He became a man. In His humanity, He had to study the Word for Himself to find out who He was. Even Jesus found Himself in the Scriptures (Isaiah 61:1-2) and then He declared it in Luke 4:17-19. "...And when he had opened the book, he found the place where it was written," Luke 4:17.

Many people have an identity crisis. They see commercials on TV and say, "I want to be like that." They think if they comb their hair like a movie star, they will be like them. They forget that people in commercials and the movies are actors who are pretending to be someone they are not.

If the devil can get you to flip flop mentally with your reasoning and your flesh, he will totally defeat you. You need to dig into the Word of God and find your identity there. You need to find out who God says you are. He knows who you are because He made you. He created you to reflect His glory! Let the Word of God establish your identity.

KNOWING YOUR TRUE IDENTITY

The devil will do everything he can to steal the Word from you and keep you from understanding your identity in Christ. The devil wants you to see yourself in the natural. He will get you to study your family tree and go generations back to find out who you are. He will try to make you think that because your mother was divorced and your grandmother was divorced, that you will end up in divorce court. He will try to tell you that because your father and your grandfather were alcoholics, that you have to be one too — after all, it runs in the family!

When you are born again, you are born into a new family. The devil will come to you saying, "Who do you think you are?" That's when you open up your Bible and read to him for a while! Say to him, "Let me tell you who I am! I have no other identity than Galatians 2:20 -- I am crucified with Christ: nevertheless I live; yet not I, but Christ liveth in me." The devil knows whether you know who you are or not.

The seven sons of Sceva tried to use the name of Jesus to cast an evil spirit out of a man without being in relationship with Jesus. The evil spirit called their bluff. "Jesus I know, and Paul I know; but who are you?" (Acts 19:15). The devil left the seven sons of Sceva "naked and wounded" because they were not identified with Christ.

Jesus identified with us when He became a man. In His humanity, He identified with us so that He could know how we feel. He knows the struggles we go through. When He went to the cross, He took our sinful condition and our curse. He sealed our identification with God there. Jesus is now at the right hand of God — forever a man — representing a new, victorious humanity for all generations.

125

A NEW, VICTORIOUS IDENTITY

If ye then be risen with Christ, seek those things which are above, where Christ sitteth on the right hand of God.

- Colossians 3:1

God initiated our identification with Christ, but we must accept it and mix our faith with it. He identified us with Himself by sending Jesus to the cross to become sin for us so we could be dead to sin. We must accept by faith our identification with Christ in His *resurrection*.

The significance of the resurrection is determined by the nature of the death. When you understand what happened on the cross - Jesus' resurrection becomes not just His victory but victory for every believer.

THE SIGNIFICANCE OF THE RESSURECTION IS DETERMINED BY THE NATURE OF THE DEATH.

Once you see yourself seated with the victorious, resurrected Christ at the right hand of the Father, you will never again identify yourself with defeat, failure, depression, fear, sickness, poverty, or lack. The truth of His triumph, which God has branded into your spirit, will cause you to declare, "I am going over, not under. I went under with Christ in His death, but now I am going over with the new identity He has given me in His resurrection. I lost my old identification, and now I have a new one. I am wearing new dog tags now, stamped with the name that is above all names!"

WHEN YOU UNDERSTAND WHAT HAPPENED ON THE CROSS - JESUS' RESURRECTION BECOMES NOT JUST HIS VICTORY BUT VICTORY FOR EVERY BELIEVER.

You are a totally different person than your mother and father made you. It does not matter who your earthly daddy is; once you are born again, God is your daddy (Romans 8:15)! This does not mean to disrespect your parents, but it means that even people who may not know who their biological parents are do not have to live their whole lives with a big gap in their soul. They can declare, "I am identified with Christ, and God is my Father. I know the family I belong to!" When you are born again, you are "re-fathered." You may have come from a dysfunctional family, but now you are part of a fully functional family — the family of God!

127

RE-CREATED IN HIS IMAGE

You can get a whole new identity when you accept who God says you are and believe you have what God says you have. God can give you a new identity. He is our "manufacturer." He is able to produce a new identity for us. We are not dealing with someone who just repairs things. We are talking about someone who makes people out of nothing! God alone is the Creator. He is the original people person.

> *Arise, and go down to the potter's house, and there I will cause thee to hear my words. Then I went down to the potter's house, and, behold, he wrought a work on the wheels. And the vessel that he made of clay was marred in the hand of the potter: so he made it again another vessel, as seemed good to the potter to make it.*
>
> *- Jeremiah 18:2-4*

God told Jeremiah, "Go down to the potter's house. I am going to show you that when people have defects in them, I can make them again!" God is in the business of remaking people. He does it from the inside out.

WHEN YOU ARE BORN AGAIN, YOU ARE RE-FATHERED BY GOD!

When you are born again, your spirit is recreated. Then God rebuilds you from the inside out by renewing your mind, and by changing your attitude and thinking. The re-creation then becomes evident by your actions. "For it is God which worketh in you both to will and to do of his good pleasure" (Philippians 2:13).

The devil would like to destroy your dignity and your self-esteem. When you see your value in the light of the price God paid for you through Christ, you will hold your head up high and forget those things which are behind. You will say of yourself, "Glory to God! That person died. I am a new creation in Christ."

EIGHT

WHO YOU ARE AND WHAT YOU HAVE IN CHRIST

System of Truth — Point Six

Wherefore henceforth we know no man after the flesh: yea though we have known Christ after the flesh, yet now henceforth know we him no more. Therefore if any man be in Christ, he is a new creature: old things are passed away; behold, all things are become new.

- 2 Corinthians 5:16,17

When anyone is united to Christ, he is a fresh Creation; the original conditions have passed away; mark! They have been replaced by new conditions.

- Wade

Therefore, if anyone is [engrafted] in Christ, the Messiah) he is a new creation (a new creature altogether); the [previous moral and spiritual condition] has passed away. Behold, the fresh and new has come!

- Amplified

...the deadliness of our former condition has passed away....

> *- Shuttle*

...and the true Christian is not merely a man altered but a man remade....

> *- Deane*

What God has done in Christ is the act of an entirely new creation. What Adam lost through disobedience was more than restored in the great plan of redemption in Christ. What does this terminology "in Christ" mean? When someone makes Jesus their Lord, they are engrafted into Him and comes into union with Him. It means that everything Satan did in Adam, God completely reversed and restored in Christ. God's work in Christ far outweighs anything done to man through Adam's fall. God did in Christ what He wanted to do in every man. When you make Jesus your Lord, God sees you in Christ. Your first birth put you in Adam and your second birth puts you in Christ.

GOD DID IN CHRIST WHAT HE WANTED TO DO IN EVERY MAN.

What is the new creation? It is something new in kind or quality, something never heard of before! We can see in 2 Corinthians 12:2 that Paul referred to himself as a man in Christ and throughout his letters everything God did for us in Christ is set to the credit of our account. There is an entirely new identification, authority, and position for a person in Christ.

Paul uses the terminology *in Christ, in Him, in whom,* or *in the Lord* around 130 times in His letters. He prayed that we would receive the spirit of wisdom and revelation in the knowledge of Him; the eyes of our understanding being enlightened; so that we would know what is the hope of His calling, what is the riches of the glory of His inheritance in the saints and what is the exceeding greatness of His power toward us who believe (Ephesians 1). I like what A.J. Gordon says in his book, *In Christ* about what God did In Christ*:*

> *No words of Scripture, if we except those, "God manifest in the flesh," hold within themselves a deeper mystery that this simple formula of the Christian life, "in Christ."*
>
> *Indeed, God's taking upon Himself humanity, and yet remaining God, is hardly more inexplicable to human thought than man's becoming a "partaker of the divine nature," and yet remaining man. Both are of those secret things that belong wholly unto God. Yet, great as is the mystery of these*

133

words, they are the key to the whole system of doctrinal mysteries. Like the famous Rosetta stone, itself a partial hieroglyph, and thereby furnishing the long-sought clew to the Egyptian hieroglyphics, these words, by their very mystery, unlock all mysteries of the divine life, letting us into secrets that were hidden from ages and from generations.

THROUGH THESE TWO WORDS, IN CHRIST, WE GET A PROFOUND INSIGHT INTO THE DIVINE METHOD OF SALVATION.

And thus, through these two words, we get a profound insight into the divine method of salvation. God does not work upon the soul by itself; bringing to bear upon it, while yet in its alienation and isolation from Him, such discipline as shall gradually render it fit to be reunited to Him. He begins rather by reuniting it to Himself, that through this union He may communicate to it that divine life and energy, without which all discipline were utterly futile. The method of grace is precisely the reverse of legalism. The latter is holiness in order to union with God; the former, union with God in order to holiness.

Nothing is more striking than the breadth of application which this principle of union with Christ has in the gospel. Christianity obliterates no natural relationship, destroys no human obligations, makes void no moral or spiritual laws. But it lifts all these up into a new sphere, and puts upon them this seal and signature of the gospel, in Christ.

NOTHING IS MORE STRIKING THAN THE BREADTH OF APPLICATION WHICH THIS PRINCIPLE OF UNION WITH CHRIST HAS IN THE GOSPEL.

Thus Christ, in taking man up into Himself, takes all that belongs to him. Instead of rending him away from his natural connections, He embraces all these with him in Himself, that He may sanctify them all. And not only is this true, but the opposite and far more wondrous fact, namely, that Christ, in raising man into union with Himself, raises him into all that belongs to Him, into his divine life, and into partnership with his divine work. So that he dies in his death; rises in his resurrection; ascends in his ascension; is seated with Him in his session at the Father's right hand; and lives in his eternal life. So marked is this latter fact, that it has led some

135

speak of the event of the Christian life as affording a striking parallel. Parallels never meet, while the very glory and mystery of believer's life is that it is one with the Saviour's and inseparable from it. It is not a life running alongside his, and taking shape and direction from it. It is his life re-enacted in his followers; the reproduction in them of those events which are immortal in energy and limitless in application.

POWERFUL PREPOSITIONS

Paul shows us how we are connected to Christ and what our relationship to Him is: He died FOR us so we died WITH Him, therefore we are now IN Him, THROUGH Him we can do all things and BY Him all our needs are supplied!

Paul uses the powerful prepositions in Christ to show you who you are and what you share with Him. Prepositions are connecting words such as for, with, in, through and by.

If I said I walked by the house you would see one picture, if I said I walked through it you would see another, or I could say I walked with it and you would see another picture altogether! The entire picture changes when I say I walk IN the house. God has completely changed our position by placing us in Christ! We look very blessed in Him. Everything Christ did in redemption has been set to the credit of the believer's account as though they did it. All we need to do is take our place in Christ!

ACKNOWLEDGE WHO YOU ARE

That the communication of thy faith may become effectual by the acknowledging of every good thing which is in you in Christ Jesus.

- Philemon 6

...full recognition and appreciation and understanding and precise knowledge of every good [thing] that is ours in [our identification with] Christ Jesus.

- Amplified

...every blessing which we have in our life in union with Christ.

- Good News Bible

I pray that everyone who meets you may catch your faith and learn from you how wonderful it is to live in Christ.

- Laubach

YOUR FAITH BECOMES CONTAGIOUS BY BEING CONSCIOUS OF EVERY GOOD THING THAT IS IN YOU IN CHRIST.

When you are in Christ, there are a lot of good things in you! Paul says we need to acknowledge those things — who we are and what we have in Christ. All of Paul's letters are centered on who we are, what we have, what God has done for us, and what we can do because we are in Christ. We are not talking about what we are going to have when we get to Heaven, but what we have now in Christ.

Paul's teaching reveals the contrast between religion and relationship. Instead of trying to achieve something in our own strength that only God could do for us, we need to agree with Him and acknowledge what He has already done. Let us look at some of the facts that are true about every believer. Let's relax in the facts of who we are and what belongs to us IN Christ!

> *Blessed be the God and Father of our Lord Jesus Christ, who hath blessed us with all spiritual blessings in heavenly places in Christ.*
>
> *- Ephesians 1:3*

But of Him are we in Christ Jesus, who of God is made unto us wisdom, righteousness, sanctification, and redemption.

- 1 Corinthians 1:30

Giving thanks unto the Father which hath made us meet to be partakers of the inheritance of the saints in light, who hath delivered us from the power of darkness and hath translated us into the kingdom of His dear Son, in whom we have redemption through His blood, even the forgiveness of sin.

- Colossians 1:12-14

And having spoiled principalities and powers, He made a show of them openly, triumphing over them in it.

- Colossians 2:15

In Him are hid all the treasures of wisdom and knowledge.

- Colossians 2:3

There is therefore now no condemnation to them which are in Christ, who walk not after the flesh, but after the Spirit. For the law of the Spirit of life in Christ Jesus has made me free from the law of sin and death.

- Romans 8:1-2

Now thanks be unto God, which always causeth us to triumph in Christ.

> *- 2 Corinthians 2:14*

But God, who is rich in mercy, for His great love wherewith He loved us, even when we were dead in sins, hath quickened us together with Christ (by grace ye are saved;) and hath raised us up together, and made us sit together in heavenly places in Christ Jesus.

> *- Ephesians 2:4-6*

Every place you see those words *in Christ, in the Lord, in the Spirit,* stop there and begin digging because there are great treasures to be found! Acknowledge or speak the same thing as God says about you and then your faith will become effectual, affecting your world around you.

John wrote in His books about the same thing, but used the Greek word zoe, or eternal life. The gospels Matthew, Mark and Luke emphasize the Kingdom of God, also used in Paul's writings. Let's see the Life of God and the Kingdom of God and how these themes flow together in Christ.

THE ZOE LIFE OF GOD

In the Gospel of John, the main theme is eternal life. In the Greek text, the word for this God-kind of life is "zoe."

Eternal life is not something you get when you die. It is something that happens to your spirit when you are born again.

The Holy Spirit breathes life, zoe, into your inner man. "He that hath the Son hath life" (1 John 5:12). Eternal life is the divine nature of God. It is a spiritual substance that is in God. It is what flows through Him, and what makes Him the way He is.

> *For as the Father hath life in himself; so hath he given to the Son to have life in himself.*
> *- John 5:26*

> *In him was life; and the life was the light of men.*
> *- John 1:4*

> *The thief cometh not, but for to steal, and to kill, and to destroy: I am come that they might have life, and that they might have it more abundantly.*
> *- John 10:10*

Jesus said, "The Father has **zoe** life in Him, and I have zoe life in me." This is what made Jesus different from everyone else on the earth. He had the very zoe life of God at work in Him. This God-kind of life produced light wherever Jesus went. That light shined in the darkness and could not be overcome (John 1:5). When you get the zoe life of God in you, you are able to be an overcomer.

> *For whatsoever is born of God overcometh the world: and this is the victory that overcometh the world, even our faith.*
>
> *- 1 John 5:4*

That God-kind of life is the power that raised Jesus from the dead. Because we were in Him, it raised us up also, and gives us power to walk in its glorious power over sin, death and the old man. Paul used this terminology when he explained man's identification and union with Christ in His death, burial and resurrection. Here is one example:

> *Therefore we are buried with Him by baptism into death: that like as Christ was raised up from the dead by the glory of the Father, even so we also should walk in newness of life.*
>
> *- Romans 6:4*

THE KINGDOM OF GOD IS WITHIN YOU

Just as the main theme of John's Gospel is eternal life (zoe), the main theme in all of Paul's letters is being in

Christ. In the Synoptic Gospels — Matthew, Mark, and Luke — the main theme is the kingdom of God. When you are born again "in Christ," you have eternal life and the kingdom of God within you (Luke 17:21).

> *Giving thanks unto the Father, which hath made us meet to be partakers of the inheritance of the saints in light: Who hath delivered us from the power of darkness, and hath translated us into the kingdom of his dear Son: In whom we have redemption through his blood, even the forgiveness of sins.*
>
> *- Colossians 1:12-14*

THE DOMINION OF GOD

The word *kingdom* has basically the same meaning as *dominion*. If you substitute the word *dominion* in each place where the word *kingdom* is used in Matthew, Mark, and Luke, you will be able to see more clearly what the kingdom of God is. John the Baptist said the dominion of God is coming. Jesus said the dominion of God is here. Paul said that you have left the power of darkness and have entered the dominion of God.

The kingdom of God is not Heaven; it is within you and it is here and now. The moment you are born again, you leave the dominion of death. You leave the authority and jurisdiction of darkness and enter a new kingdom where Satan no longer has dominion over you. When Adam sinned, he lost his dominion. When Jesus came, He restored dominion.

> *For if by one man's offense death reigned by one; much more they which receive abundance of grace and of the gift of righteousness shall reign in life by one, Jesus Christ.*
>
> *- Romans 5:17*

Ben Campbell Johnson's paraphrase translates the kingdom of God as the "Spirit dimension." John 4:24 says, "God is a Spirit." The kingdom of God would have to be a spirit dimension. What God has done for you in Christ is who you are in your spirit — it launches you into the realm of God. Your spirit, joined to Christ, can receive spiritual blessings. You do not have to go to Heaven to have Heaven in your life.

THE WORD OF FAITH IS NIGH THEE

> *The word is nigh thee, even in thy mouth, and in thy heart: that is, the word of faith, which we preach.*
>
> *- Romans 10:8*

The dominion of God is as close as your heart and your mouth — it is within you. Paul was saying that you do not have to ascend to the right hand of God to bring Jesus down. You do not have to descend into the deep to bring Christ up. You do not have to go to Tulsa, Toronto, or Los Angeles to get the blessings of God. The kingdom of God is within you. All you have to do is get the Word of God in your mouth and in your heart. You have passed from death to life. The life of God is inside of you!

YOU DON'T HAVE TO WAIT TO GO TO HEAVEN TO HAVE THE LIFE OF HEAVEN.

Do not try to get a hold of the kingdom of God with your head or your flesh. Get a hold of it with your inner man, your spirit. Reach out and say, "I am in Christ, and Christ lives in me. I am in the kingdom of God, and the kingdom of God is in me. I have eternal life, and the eternal life of God is in me." Do not keep your boat in dry dock — get into the river! The river of living water flows from the kingdom of God. Romans 14:17 says that the kingdom of God is "...righteousness, peace, and joy in the Holy Ghost."

Perfect Union with the Master
He's the Vine and I'm the branch
He was wounded; I was engrafted
Perfect union with the Lord

He's the Head and I'm His body
He became sin just for me
And I passed from death to His life
Where I live eternally

Now I reign with Him forever
Enthroned far above
Every name and all dominion
And He's wrapped me in His love

- Trina Hankins

If you are not impressed with who you are in Christ you have not seen Him lately! "The fullness of the Godhead bodily dwelleth in Him. And you are complete in Him who is the head of all principality," Colossians 2:9,10. The Amplified Bible says, "In Christ you too are filled with the Godhead—Father, Son, and Holy Spirit."

IF YOU ARE NOT IMPRESSED WITH WHO YOU ARE IN CHRIST YOU HAVE NOT SEEN HIM LATELY!

He that is joined unto the Lord is one spirit.

- 1 Corinthians 6:17

He who is in union with the Master is one with Him in spirit.

- Weymouth

But he who unites himself with the Master forms a single spirit.

- Authentic

But if you give yourself to the Lord, you and Christ are joined together as one person.

- The Living Bible

NINE

WHAT JESUS IS DOING NOW
System of Truth — Point Seven

And hath put all things under His feet, and gave him to be the head over all things to the church, which is His body, the fullness of him that filleth all in all.

- Ephesians 1:22,23

Jesus put aside His glory, became a man, and lived on the earth as a member of the human race for thirty-three years. That was not the end of His identification with mankind. Jesus suffered as a man, died as a man, and is now a resurrected man seated at the right hand of God the Father.

God is now our Father as well as our Creator, and Jesus is the firstborn of the family of God. Throughout all eternity, the only begotten Son of God will remain fully God and fully man. There is an eternal union between God and man because Jesus fully identified with us.

> *But God, who is rich in mercy, for his great love*
> *wherewith he loved us, Even when we were dead*
> *in sins, hath quickened us together with Christ,*
> *(by grace ye are saved;) And hath raised us up*
> *together, and made us sit together in heavenly*
> *places in Christ Jesus:*
>
> *- Ephesians 2:4-6*

Jesus is the express image of the Father God, the outshining of His glory, "...The perfect imprint and very image of [God's] nature," (Hebrews 1:3). Jesus, according to the perfect will of God, is still actively working for our good to save us to the uttermost by ever living to make intercession for us. He is also our Mediator, our High Priest, and the Shepherd and Guardian of our souls.

JESUS OUR HIGH PRIEST

Jesus has obtained a more excellent ministry. If you kept the Old Covenant, God guaranteed that He would bless you coming in and going out (Deuteronomy 28:6). He guaranteed that He would forgive all your iniquities and heal all your diseases (Psalm 103:3).

> *He brought them forth also with silver and gold:*
> *and there was not one feeble person among their*
> *tribes.*
>
> *- Psalm 105:37*

Some people say, "But that was in the Old Testament and it was just for Israel. That's not for us today." Actually, these promises were made to those who would not fear but believe — for those who would have faith. The Bible says that Abraham believed God and it was counted to him as righteousness (Romans 4:22).

Even so, we have a better covenant. Paul would not call it better unless it included at least as much as the Old Covenant. Righteousness has not just been imputed to us, but we have been made the righteousness of God in Christ. We have received eternal life — the life and nature of God. Our bodies have become the temples of the Holy Ghost (1 Corinthians 3:16).

> *God, who at sundry times and in divers manners spake in time past unto the fathers by the prophets, Hath in these last days spoken unto us by his Son.*
>
> *- Hebrews 1:1,2*

Paul was saying that what the prophets spoke to us about in the Old Testament was fulfilled in the New Testament in Christ. He said in Galatians 3:24-26 that the Law was our schoolmaster to bring us to Christ (Galatians 3:24-26) and now we are living in the reality of all that God promised Abraham. He exhorted them to stand fast in the liberty in Christ and to not be entangled again with the yoke of bondage to the Law (Galatians 5:1). He had set forth Christ crucified and they received the Spirit by the hearing of faith and not by the works of the Law (Galatians 3:12).

In the letter to the Hebrews, Paul was writing to Jewish Christians who wanted to go back to the Old Covenant under the Law. Paul told them, "You don't want to go back! Jesus is a better spokesman, a better priest, and a better sacrifice. In the Old Testament the sacrifices for sin had to be made year after year. In Hebrews 10:12, Jesus entered into the holy place with His blood, and made the sacrifice for sin once and for all!" The sacrifice for sin will never have to be made again because the blood of Jesus obtained eternal redemption for us.

> *But now hath He obtained a more excellent ministry, by how much he is the Mediator of a better covenant, which was established upon better promises.*
>
> *- Hebrews 8:6*

Under the Old Covenant, the high priest carried out in detail every part of the covenant given to Moses such as sacrifices, intercession and worship, guiding the people, releasing blessings and the mediation of the covenant. It wasn't perfect and had to be repeated yearly. Under the New Covenant, we see that Jesus, the Head of the Church, our Savior and Friend, is also our High Priest, once for all time. We see that provision has been made through God's great redemption plan to bring us into His Presence.

> *Having therefore, brethren, boldness to enter the Holiest by the blood of Jesus, by a new and living way, which He consecrated for us through the veil, that is, through His flesh, and having a High Priest over the house of God, let us draw near with a true heart in full assurance of faith, having our hearts sprinkled from an evil conscience and our bodies washed with pure water.*
> *- Hebrews 10:19-22*

> *Christ came as a High Priest of the good things to come, with the greater and more perfect tabernacle not made with hands, that is, not of this creation. Not by the blood of goats and calves, but with his own blood, He entered once into the Holy Place once for all, having obtained eternal redemption...how much more shall the blood of Christ, who through the eternal Spirit offered Himself without spot to God, cleanse*

> *your conscience from dead works to serve the*
> *living God? And for this reason He is the*
> *Mediator of the new covenant....*
>
> > *- Hebrews 9:11,12,14,15*

In His redemptive work, Jesus opened Heaven to all who are washed in His blood. We have entered into His body and are now in union with Him. The first thing we see in His Holy Place is Him, our High Priest. We feel the cleansing effects of the sprinkling of the blood upon our conscience. We see our Mediator washing us with pure water as He sanctifies and cleanses us with the washing of water by the Word so that we can be a glorious church, not having spot or wrinkle or any such thing, but that the church should be holy and without blemish (Ephesians 5:26, 27). He put away sin once for all as our High Priest — once for all. He justified, sanctified and glorified us by His sacrifice (Hebrews 9:24-27; Romans 8:30).

FOR THE ENJOYMENT OF THIS BLESSEDNESS, NOTHING IS NECESSARY EXCEPT FAITH IN THE BLOOD. THE BLOOD ALONE HAS DONE EVERYTHING.
- ANDREW MURRAY

Jesus fulfilled every detail of the covenant and with His death activated the new will and testament forever. His blood is ever before the Father and cries for mercy, grace and victory as He mediates His Covenant, the better covenant, based on better promises! Jesus Himself has become the guarantee or surety of a better covenant.

> *By so much was Jesus made a surety of a better testament.*
>
> > *- Hebrews 7:22*

> *In keeping with [the oath's greater strength and force], Jesus has become the Guarantee of a better (stronger) agreement [a more excellent and more advantageous covenant].*
>
> > *- Amplified*

JESUS, OUR INTERCESSOR AND SAVIOR

> *Wherefore He is able to save to the uttermost them that come unto God by him, seeing he ever liveth to make intercession for them.*
>
> > *- Hebrews 7:25*

> *He can save to the utmost limit of completeness....*
>
> > *- Wand*

Jesus is able to save us to the uttermost. I like to say from the guttermost to the uttermost! The work He has begun, He will finish. He knew you before you ever thought about Him and has a plan for your victory in every battle! What He has started, He will finish — not just halfway, not thirty percent, not seventy-five percent, but completely!

Jesus is your Savior and is well able to save you. The word *save* or *salvation* in the Greek is the same word as deliverance, safety, healing, preservation and soundness. He is able to save completely — to the uttermost!

Jesus lives in Heaven where as a High Priest, He is praying continually, ever interceding to the Father for the Church. We have some of His prayers in John 17 and in the letters written to the Church, so we have insight into what He is praying for. He desires for us to walk in truth, be fruitful, be enlightened, to walk worthy, to be grounded and grow in His love, and strengthened and filled with His glory. It is good to take His prayers and pray them as He spoke them.

> *Inasmuch then as we have a great High Priest Who has [already] ascended and passed through the heavens, Jesus the Son of God, let us hold fast our confession [of faith in Him]. For we do not have a High Priest Who is unable to understand and sympathize and have a shared feeling with our weaknesses and infirmities and liability to*

the assaults of temptations, but One Who has been tempted in every respect as we are, yet without sinning. Let us hold fast then fearlessly and confidently and boldly draw near to the throne of grace (the throne of God's unmerited favor to us sinners), that we may receive mercy [for our failures] and find grace to help in good time for every need [appropriate help and well-timed help, coming just when we need it].

- Hebrews 4:14-16 Amplified

Christ has given us a better covenant based upon better promises. He obtained a better ministry. As High Priest, He understands the temptations, struggles, and the difficulties that we face in this life. He understands our weaknesses. This gives us confidence to go to the Father and look to Jesus, the Author and Finisher, or Perfecter of our faith (Hebrews 12:2). He is the One who knows us and our needs better than we do. As we go before the throne of grace to get God's help, we know we can come boldly because Jesus is our Savior and Advocate. Jesus' new job is to represent us.

Jesus ever lives to pray for us! He is the head and we are His body so He is touched with our feelings and weaknesses. We are joined together, one with Him, so that means we can join Him in His session at the right hand of

God. With the help of the Holy Spirit, we are able to pray a perfect prayer and make powerful requests in His faith and see His will come to the earth. As we hold fast to His Covenant, the Holy Spirit will helps us to pray and make intercession according to the will of God (Romans 8:26-27). It is Christ that died, and furthermore is risen, who is even at the right hand of God, who also makes intercession for us (Romans 8:34).

JESUS OUR ADVOCATE

> *Be sober, be vigilant; because your adversary the devil, as a roaring lion, walketh about, seeking whom he may devour.*
>
> *- 1 Peter 5:8*

The Bible tells us to be on our guard, to be watchful and attentive because we have an adversary. Your adversary the devil is constantly trying to gain access into your thought life, your marriage, your family, your finances, and your future.

SATAN IS THE ACCUSER OF THE BRETHREN - JESUS IS THE ADVOCATE!

The Greek word for adversary is *antidikos*, which simply means a lawyer who argues in court or it means a prosecutor. The book of Revelation refers to Satan as the accuser of the brethren. He will bring up all of your thoughts, all of your failures and weaknesses, and proceed to prosecute you. He will constantly point out every little thing you didn't do or everything you should have done. He is the accuser and that is what he does best. He will bring you before the Judge and he will actually use facts against you. He will use facts of past sins, and past mistakes, to bring you into a place where he can devour you. He uses just enough facts to make you sabotage your own future with your own thinking and talking. However, the devil never tells the rest of the story. This is why we must come to understand the Word of God.

You must realize who your adversary is and how he works. In 2 Corinthians 2:11, Paul says "...we are not ignorant of his devices." Another meaning of the word *devices* translated from the Greek is mind. We are not ignorant of his mind schemes. The devil's biggest tool is to play mind games.

WHEN JESUS IS HANDLING YOUR CASE YOU CANNOT LOSE. IN FACT, JESUS HAS NEVER LOST A CASE.

The devil could never sell his stuff if he weren't camouflaged. He brings condemnation, guilt, and all kinds of feelings and puts pressure on you and on your emotions. Then, he will get you to move out of line with the Word. The devil is the tempter and the accuser. He will tempt you to do what is wrong. Then after you do it, he will accuse you and condemn you.

> *My little children, these things write I unto you, that ye sin not. And if any man sin, we have an advocate with the Father, Jesus Christ the righteous.*
>
> *- 1 John 2:1*

The difference between Jesus and the devil is that the devil is the accuser and Jesus is the advocate. As an advocate He is our lawyer. One translation says, He is the one that pleads your case for you. This is where Jesus comes in; and He will always tell the rest of the story. The rest of the story is that He has pardoned you of every sin, every crime, every thought, and purged you with His blood. When Jesus is handling your case you cannot lose. In fact, Jesus has never lost a case.

> *But if we walk in the light as he is in the light, we have fellowship with one another, and the blood of Jesus Christ His Son cleanses us from all sin. If we confess our sins, He is faithful and just to forgive us our sins and to cleanse us from all unrighteousness.*
>
> *- 1 John 1:7,9*

Your advocate will tell you to plead the Blood of Jesus and tap into His mercy and grace. He will anoint you with fresh oil and strengthen you to stand up and resist the devil by speaking His Word. He is your lawyer in Heaven and He is on your side. If God be for you, who can be against you!

JESUS THE HIGH PRIEST OF YOUR CONFESSION

> *Wherefore, holy brethren, partakers of the heavenly calling, consider the Apostle and High Priest of our profession, Christ Jesus.*
>
> *- Hebrews 3:1*

Look at the words *Apostle* and *High Priest*. The word *Apostle* means a sent one, or one sent to establish something. A *High Priest* is one who represents someone else. Jesus was sent to establish everything His blood purchased for us and represent everybody His blood has redeemed.

The only way He can do His job is through our profession. The word *profession* is the same Greek word as *confession*. Jesus can only do His job when we say something. He represents our confession before the Father God. Confess with your mouth that His Word is true no matter what the circumstances around you look like. He

161

is waiting for you to acknowledge that He has already redeemed you — you are delivered and have been made righteous in Him.

It is important for the body of Christ to carry out the divine commands of Jesus, the Head of the Church. He instructed us in Matthew 18:19, that whatever we bind on earth will be bound in Heaven, and whatever we loose on earth will be loosed in Heaven. Some things will never change until the church takes our authority on the earth. When we do, He will watch over His Word to perform it (Jeremiah 1:12). He is the Apostle and High Priest of our confession.

> *But in these last days He has spoken to us in [the person of a] Son, Whom He appointed heir and lawful Owner of all things, also by and through Whom He created the worlds and the reaches of space and the ages of time [He made, produced built, operated, and arranged them in order]. He is the sole expression of the glory of God [the Light-being, the out-raying or radiance of the divine], image of God's nature, upholding and maintaining and guiding and propelling the universe by His mighty word of power....*
>
> *- Hebrews 1:2,3 Amplified*

162

Whenever we get in the Spirit we can hear what He is saying. When we read the Word and the Holy Spirit breathes it to life in our spirits, we then take hold of it, praying in the Spirit. The dunamis power of God is released against every obstacle, lifting up a standard against the enemy and causing the creative will of God to come to pass!

JESUS OUR SHEPHERD

Now may the God of Peace who brought up our Lord Jesus from the dead, that great Shepherd of the sheep, through the blood of the everlasting covenant, make you complete in every good work to do His will, working in you what is well pleasing in His sight, through Jesus Christ.

- Hebrews 13:20,21

Jesus is also the Great Shepherd of the sheep. He is the Head of the Church, and we are His body. That means the directives for the body of Christ come from the head of the body — Jesus. He is the Great Shepherd whose voice we know and follow. Psalm 23 deals with what Jesus is doing for you right now — the ministry of the Great Shepherd.

163

The Lord is my shepherd; I shall not want. He maketh me to lie down in green pastures: he leadeth me beside the still waters. He restoreth my soul: he leadeth me in the paths of righteousness for his name's sake. Yea, though I walk through the valley of the shadow of death, I will fear no evil: for thou art with me; thy rod and thy staff they comfort me. Thou preparest a table before me in the presence of mine enemies: thou anointest my head with oil; my cup runneth over. Surely goodness and mercy shall follow me all the days of my life: and I will dwell in the house of the Lord forever.

What a wonderful Shepherd! Peter calls Him the Shepherd and Guardian of our souls (1 Peter 2:25). He tells us that when the Chief Shepherd is revealed, we will win the conqueror's crown of glory (1 Peter 5:4)!

JESUS IS PRONOUNCING THE BLESSING

The Lord bless you and keep you; The Lord make his face to shine upon you , and be gracious to you The Lord lift up His countenance upon you and give you peace.

- Numbers 6:24-26

In the Old Covenant, God guaranteed that He would bless you coming in and going out (Deuteronomy 28:6). After giving the Great Commission and commanding the disciples to be filled with the Holy Spirit, Jesus lifted up His hands to bless the disciples. While He was blessing them, He parted from them and was carried up into Heaven (Luke 24:50,51). Jesus entered into the role of a High Priest over the Church and one of His ministries now is to release the blessing. In the Old Covenant, one of the duties of the priest were to pronounce blessing.

> *Blessed be the God and Father of our Lord Jesus Christ, who hath blessed us with all spiritual blessings in heavenly places in Christ.*
>
> *- Ephesians 1:3*

T E N

HOW TO GROW UP IN CHRIST
System of Truth — Point Eight

As ye have therefore received Christ Jesus the
Lord, so walk ye in Him: rooted and built up in
Him and established in the faith, as ye have been
taught, abounding therein with thanksgiving.

- Colossians 2:6,7

When our children and grandchildren were born, one of the most important things that demanded attention was their nourishment. This care of the babies would begin to establish a pattern of eating and growing. There were always questions about how much they ate and weighed. If they were crying, the first question asked was if they were hungry or needed changing. I would say, "Feed that baby quick!" One of our grandsons had a problem eating during the first days and how happy we were when he got established in a routine and began to grow!

167

Much of the letters to the Church deal with being established in faith and growing up spiritually. Then we become productive, full grown Christians who look, talk and act like Christ. How did you get saved and receive Him? By hearing the Gospel, believing it in your heart and confessing with your mouth Jesus is Lord. That is faith. Faith involves hearing, believing and speaking what you believe.

> *That if thou shall confess with thy mouth the Lord Jesus, and shall believe with thine heart that God hath raised Him from the dead, thou shalt be saved. For with the heart man believeth unto righteousness; and with the mouth confession is made unto salvation.*
>
> *- Romans 10:9,10*

In this chapter we will see how to renew our minds and feed our faith by meditation in God's Word **(Section 1)**, how to be strengthened spiritually through prayer and fellowshipping with God **(Section 2)** and the necessity of being in your place in the Body of Christ **(Section 3)**. Paul emphasizes how important this link in the chain of his System of Truth is so that we can carry faith from generation to generation and fulfill the Great Commission of Jesus.

S E C T I O N   O N E
THE WORD OF GOD

RENEW YOUR MIND

I beseech you therefore, brethren, by the mercies of God, that ye present your bodies a living sacrifice, holy, acceptable unto God, which is your reasonable service. And be not conformed to this world: but be ye transformed by the renewing of your mind, that ye may prove what is that good, and acceptable, and perfect, will of God.

- Romans 12:1-2

The renewing of your mind is a continual, lifetime process. The day will never come when you will be able to say, "Okay, I've done that, now my mind is renewed." You need to renew your mind throughout your entire lifetime by daily feeding on the Word.

Since you have heard about Jesus and have learned the truth that comes from him, throw off your old sinful nature and your former way of

> *life, which is corrupted by lust and deception. Instead, let the Spirit renew your thoughts and attitudes. Put on your new nature, created to be like God - truly righteous and holy.*
>
> *- Ephesians 4:21-24 TLB*

When you are born again, you become a new creature in Christ. You become a new man on the inside, but there is evidence that the old man was there. The evidence is in your mind, your thinking, your reasoning, your opinions, your traditions, your emotions, your conduct, and your behavior.

THE RENEWING OF YOUR MIND IS A CONTINUAL, LIFETIME PROCESS.

When my grandfather (who we called Pop) died, we attended his funeral, went to the cemetery where they lowered him into the ground and then went back to the house where he and Granny had been living to eat and fellowship. As I looked around, I saw all the evidence that Pop had lived there (his bed, clothes, pictures, glasses, etc.) were lying around, but Pop was gone! He would never live there again because he had died and was buried and all that was left of him was the memories.

After a period of time, I came back to visit Granny and everything looked very different because she and my mother had gone through all the drawers, closets, the garage and the entire house. They had gathered all of his belongings together and had gotten rid of them. All that was left were a few pictures and items to remember him by.

That is how it is when you get saved. The old man is gone — dead and buried, but you still have evidence he was there. You have all of this old man junk lying around, but you do not have to get up every morning and kill the old man. He is truly gone!

> *...reckon ye also yourselves to be dead indeed unto sin....*
>
> *- Romans 6:11*

You are to reckon, or consider to be true, that you died with Christ, were buried with Him, and were raised with Him. Then sin shall no longer have dominion over you. As you reckon it to be so, evidence of the old man's existence will begin to disappear.

We are in a world where even many Christians still think like their old man and keep many of the values from their old nature. They do not want to get rid of their "old" stuff because their flesh likes it. They want to keep a few

171

memories and hang on to some old habits and attitudes. Instead, they need to haul off some things like lying, anger, stealing, and corrupt communication.

> *This we know — that our old self was nailed to the cross with Him, in order that our sinful nature might be deprived of its power.*
>
> *- Romans 6:6 Weymouth*

Part of going on with a new life is marking the spot where the old one died! We have been crucified with Christ, the old man is dead and now it is no longer I but Christ who is living in me!

RENOVATING YOUR MIND

Your soul has stored memories, experiences, events, failures, disappointments, hurts, bruises, intellectual ideas, and reasoning. It's like a warehouse! You have all this "baggage" in your soul and it all needs to be restored.

Paul speaks of renewing your mind in Romans 12:2. The Machievelle translation says, "...to renovate your mind." The Knox translation says, "Remake your mind."

A few years ago, I restored an old truck. I thought I could do it for about $5,000, but once I started working on it, I discovered that a panel was rusted out. I knew I had a choice to either replace the panel or paint over it. If I just painted over it, in a year or so, the rust would break out and ruin the whole paint job.

Many times people decide, "I'm a busy person, and I do not have time to meditate on the Word. I do not have time to pray in the Holy Ghost, so let's just have a little meeting and I'll run around the church." In essence they are just painting over the rust.

The anointing breaks the yoke of any bondage the devil has put on you (Isaiah 10:27) and gives you the freedom to renovate your soul. The anointing breaks the control of the enemy, but you still have to receive the engrafted Word which is able to save your soul. That means there is a process to renovation.

RECEIVE THE ENGRAFTED WORD

...lay aside all filthiness and superfluity of naughtiness, receive with meekness the engrafted word, which is able to save your souls.
- James 1:21

To receive the Word with meekness means to be teachable. You must have an attitude that accepts the Word as final authority. You must have a hunger for the

Word and pay attention to the Word. An attitude of meekness and getting the Word engrafted in you are two parts of a whole; you cannot get the Word engrafted in you if you do not receive it with the right attitude. James 1:21 says that the engrafted Word is able to save your soul.

When the Word is properly engrafted, behavior will change. If you are having trouble with a behavior or attitude, go back to the Word and let it be engrafted in your heart and receive it with meekness. The ability to save your soul is in the Word. The anointing will help you, but you will have to receive the engrafted Word through a daily process of meditating on it.

You can engraft entire chapters of the Bible on the inside of you, such as 1 Corinthians 13, Isaiah 53, Psalm 23, and Romans 6 and 8. You can take all the redemption scriptures, prosperity scriptures, and healing scriptures and get them engrafted on the inside of you. When the devil comes, the Word is already working in you and will raise up a standard against him!

REDEEMED FROM ALL INIQUITY

Who gave Himself for us, that He might redeem us from all iniquity....

-Titus 2:14

...that He might cut us loose from every evil habit....

-Jordan

Jesus gave Himself to redeem us from all iniquity. Iniquity is sin, but it is more than just an act of sin. Iniquity is an evil tendency or habit, a weakness in your character, a continual thing that is going on in some area of your life. It may have come into your life by something that has happened to you. The attitudes, habits, and iniquity of those you live with or hang around can creep in and pollute you as well.

Your parents may have had the same problem with iniquity. This is why people will say, "His daddy was an alcoholic, now he is one!" "Her parents were divorced. Come to think of it, so were her grandparents. I guess she was bound to be divorced too!" These things are generational iniquity problems. They can continue to mess up an entire family, generation after generation until the blood of Jesus breaks them.

If there is iniquity, a tendency toward sin, in some area of your life, you can get it repaired, renewed, restored, and changed by receiving with humility the Word of God as the supreme and final authority on the subject. The engrafted Word will make the real changes on the inside of you. Feed on what God has done for you in Christ. Begin to declare, "I am who God says I am, I have what God says I have, and I can do what God says I can do!"

You are a new creation in Christ when you are born again. God becomes your Father, and iniquity does not run in His family. Even if you were abused or something happened in your family to pollute or affect you in some way, it has no right to dominate you or your children any longer once you become a new creature in Christ.

The Word says, Jesus gave Himself for us to redeem us from all iniquity (Titus 2:14), and that He has redeemed us from the curse of the law (Galatians 3:13). The Word also says that He has delivered us from the power of darkness (Colossians 1:13). In John 14:30, Jesus said, "The prince of this world cometh, and hath nothing in me." Another translation says, "He has no place to get a hold of me." When you are born again you can say, "The devil is coming after me, but he can't get hold of me anywhere because Christ has redeemed me from all iniquity."

One of the first places the devil will attack is in the mind. In Genesis 3:13, Eve said, "The serpent beguiled me...." Years ago, I read a translation which said, "The serpent made me forget." The devil will "beguile" or show you a pretty picture. Unless you are meditating on the Word, you will forget what God says.

> *(For the weapons of our warfare are not carnal, but mighty through God to the pulling down of strong holds;) Casting down imaginations, and every high thing that exalteth itself against the knowledge of God, and bringing into captivity every thought to the obedience of Christ.*
>
> *- 2 Corinthians 10:4,5*

> *...we take captive and render submissive to the Christ every defiant thought.*
>
> *- 2 Corinthians 10:5 - Wade*

Paul said, "Neither give place to the devil" (Ephesians 4:27). If you start thinking in line with fear, then you actually give the devil a place to work in your life. Fear is faith in reverse. Do not allow fear to set in. Take those thoughts captive that do not measure up against the standard of the Word!

The devil may also come against you with thoughts of condemnation like, "You'll never amount to anything. What makes you think you will ever be able to do anything significant?" Those thoughts did not come from God. They are not in the Bible. Remember what Paul said in Romans 8:1, *"There is therefore now no condemnation to them which are in Christ Jesus, who walk not after the flesh, but after the Spirit."*

You need to capture thoughts that do not line up with God's Word. If the devil can get you under condemnation, shame, or guilt, he can cheat you out of your inheritance.

THE ART OF MEDITATION

Meditate upon these things; give thyself wholly to them; that thy profiting may appear to all.
- 1 Timothy 4:15

I like what Norman Vincent Peale said, "It seems there is an invisible reservoir of abundance which can be tapped by obeying certain spiritual laws." In difficult times people search out resources to sustain themselves. Those who put their trust in God and learn to tap into His supply will not lack and will even flourish.

IT SEEMS THERE IS AN INVISIBLE RESERVOIR OF ABUNDANCE WHICH CAN BE TAPPED BY OBEYING CERTAIN SPIRITUAL LAWS.

There is an art of meditation upon God's Word which draws out His wisdom and His supernatural power to

178

produce amazing results. Meditation is often overlooked and skipped as we go through the daily affairs of life; it's important to study how to meditate and what to meditate on in order to see the results of Christian meditation.

> *But his delight is in the law of the Lord; and in His law doth he meditate day and night; and He shall be like a tree that's planted by the rivers of water, that bringeth forth his fruit in his season; his leaf also shall not wither and whatsoever he doeth shall prosper.*
>
> *- Psalm 1:2,3 KJV*

> *You thrill to God's Word, you chew on Scripture day and night. You're a tree replanted in Eden, bearing fresh fruit every month, never dropping a leaf, always in blossom.*
>
> *- Message Bible*

> *Most blessed is the man who believes in, trusts in, and relies on the Lord, and whose hope and confidence the Lord is. For he shall be like a tree planted by the waters that spreads out its roots by the river; and it shall not see and fear when heat comes; but its leaf shall be green, It shall not be anxious and full of care in the year of drought, nor shall it cease yielding fruit.*
>
> *Jeremiah 17:7,8 Amplified*

He is like a tree planted along the riverbank, with its roots reaching deep into the water — a tree not bothered by the heat nor worried by long months of drought. Its leaves stay green....

- Taylor

Most blessed is the man who trusts me, God, the woman who sticks with God. They're like trees replanted in Eden, putting down roots near the rivers — Never a worry through the hottest of summers, never dropping a leaf, serene and calm through droughts, bearing fresh fruit every season.

- Message Bible

He is like a tree by the water side that thrusts its roots to the stream: when the heat comes it feels no alarm, its foliage stays green; it has no worries in the year of drought, and never ceases to bear fruit.

- Jerusalem

In 1 Timothy 4:15, Paul said to "meditate upon these things; give thyself wholly to them, that thy profiting may appear to all." When a tree is well watered, it is evident to all because you can see the fruit and the green leaves. In the same way, those around you can see the results of the Word working in your life. The fruit of blessing, health and peace is very tangible!

HOW TO MEDITATE

The dictionary defines the word meditate as this: to talk with yourself, mutter, cogitate; it is an inward and outward conversation; it means to study, chew over, think over, ponder, excogitate, muse, reflect, mull over, speculate. The word cogitate means to think deeply, think out, think up, dream up, and to hatch. Excogitate is to invent; create mentally. Christian meditation is NOT sitting on the floor with your legs crossed, humming to yourself and emptying your mind. You cannot have a relationship with God without having a relationship with the Word of God.

YOU CANNOT HAVE A RELATIONSHIP WITH GOD WITHOUT HAVING A RELATIONSHIP WITH THE WORD OF GOD.

If you know how to worry or if you have been offended, then you know how to meditate. You constantly think about what could happen, what is happening and speculate about the results. It even affects your body and emotions! The Bible originated in the East where the culture is given to meditation and it has much to say about this exercise. Philippians 4:6,7 says not to worry about anything, but to turn those worries into requests followed by thanksgiving.

God promises to surround your heart with His peace. According to verse 8, our part is to do something with our thoughts. We are to meditate or think about things that are true, honest, just, pure, lovely, of good report, virtuous, and begin praising instead of worrying.

> *According as His divine power has given unto us all things that pertain to life and godliness, through the knowledge of him that hath called us to glory and virtue: whereby are given unto us exceeding great and precious promises; that by these ye might be partakers of the divine nature, having escaped the corruption that is in the world through lust.*
>
> *- 2 Peter 1:3,4*

As Christians, we do not have to participate in the corruption around us. There is an escape! Because of the new birth, you are a partaker of God's divine nature and have in you everything you need to overcome in life. Through meditation, the Word becomes engrafted in you and is able to save or restore your soul which is your mind, will and emotions (James 1:21). When you are speaking the Word of God, pondering, muttering, turning it over, digesting, and dreaming about all of these great promises that are given to you, you begin to draw up divine power, just like a tree draws water out of the soil it is planted in.

WHO ARE YOU WEARING?

While I was watching the Academy Awards on television, I listened to the announcers interviewing the actresses and discussing the beautiful designer gowns that the ladies were wearing. I noticed the announcers asked the ladies WHO they were wearing? Really they were asking the name of the designer — Versace, Oscar de la Renta, etc. As Christians, we must understand that we are to clothe ourselves with Christ. We must put on or clothe ourselves with the garments of praise and robes of righteousness!

When a Christian meditates on who they are in Christ and allows the Holy Spirit to clothe them with power from Heaven, they are putting on or wearing Christ. In Ephesians 4:23,24, Paul said, "be renewed in the spirit of your mind...put on the new man, which is created in righteousness and true holiness." Again, Paul says in

Romans 13:14, "put ye on the Lord Jesus Christ, and make not provision for the flesh, to fulfill the lusts thereof."

You should not be wearing your old identity. God has designed new clothes for you to put on. Put on the consciousness of your redemption and who you are in Christ. People around you will be able to see Jesus' love, joy, peace, ability, and wisdom. You will bring glory to Him and people will ask, "Who are you wearing?"

FEAST ON THE WORD

> *Your words were found and I did eat them and they were to me the joy and rejoicing of my heart.*
>
> *- Jeremiah 15:16*

> *When your words showed up, I ate them - swallowed them whole. What a feast!*
>
> *- Message Bible*

> *When your words came, I devoured them:*
>
> *- Jerusalem Bible*

> *Your words are what sustained me, they are food to my soul.*
>
> *- Taylor*

My mother was the slowest eater I have ever known. We would start our meal together and two hours later she would still be chewing! I would tell her to take the rest home because I had things to do! She would then tell me the benefits of eating slowly. Doctors say you should chew your food 32 times before swallowing and that digestion begins in your mouth where the food is broken down before you swallow.

God's Word is faith food and is meant to be eaten. "Man shall not live by bread alone, but by every word that proceedeth out of the mouth of God," Matthew 4:4. Faith comes by hearing and hearing by the Word of God and it has to be digested for faith to come. When you meditate, the Word gets in your eyes, your ears, your mouth and then into all of your body.

In Mark 4, Jesus taught the importance of hearing the Word and compared it to seed. The most important thing was for the roots of the seed to go down into the soil, causing growth and eventually fruit to come forth. Wherever you have a need in your life, begin to gather seeds of the Word so that you can plant them in your heart and grow a crop of healing, peace, finances, your family's salvation, etc. 1 Corinthians 3:6 says, "I have planted, Apollos watered; but God gave the increase."

The planting occurs when you first hear the Word and then it must be watered by repetition. Some reject the watering process and get no results from the Word they heard. If there is no increase, check out your watering or your meditation of the Word. Proverbs 4:20-22 instructs us to keep the Word in our mouth, before our eyes and in our heart. When we do this, health is the result. Take it just like you would take medicine. He wants you to be well because He sent His Word to heal you (Psalm 107:20)!

DELIGHT IN THE LAW OF THE LORD

David said his delight was in the Law of the Lord. What are those laws? They are His Word. They are the Law of Faith (Romans 3:27), the Law of Love (1 Corinthians 13), the Law of the Spirit of Life (Romans 8:2), and the Law of Sowing and Reaping (2 Corinthians 9:6-11). Every Christian must be personally responsible to tap into the power of God in these areas in order to live above the corruption in the world. Psalm 119, the longest chapter in the Bible, overflows with David's love for God's Word. He mentions meditation seven times. When you sing psalms like David, it is a form of meditation. He said, "I will sing unto the Lord as long as I live: I will sing praise to my God while I have my being. My meditation of him shall be sweet: I will be glad in the Lord," Psalm 104:33,34.

GOD IS CLOSER THAN YOU THINK!

There are warning signs on some rearview mirrors that say, "the objects in the mirror are much closer than they appear." God is closer to you than you realize and when you acknowledge Him, He will respond to you! When Paul was in Athens, he addressed the philosophers there on Mars' Hill who had an altar to the Unknown God. He told them about the God who made the Heaven and earth and how that if they would seek Him they would find Him. "...He be not far from every one of us: For in him we live, and move, and have our being...For we are also His offspring," Acts 17:27,28. God is not far from you and when you call on Jesus, when you acknowledge Him and His Word, you will tap into His Presence.

WHATEVER PART OF THE BIBLE YOU GET THRILLED ABOUT IS WHAT WILL WORK FOR YOU.

As you meditate on Hebrews 10:19-22, the Holy Spirit will paint a vivid picture of how, through the Blood of Jesus, you have access with boldness into His throne room. God's Word will begin to flood your consciousness. You will have tapped into that great reservoir of abundance, love and unlimited grace. You will have the mind of Christ.

187

You will enter the realm where all things are possible. Whatever part of the Bible you get thrilled about is what will work for you. It will walk off the page and into your heart, living and abiding in you, guiding you every step of the way, every night and day. Fall in love with it! Eat it! Delight in it! Speak it! Sing it! Shout it!

S E C T I O N   T W O
THE POWER OF PRAYER

THE ART OF PRAYER

Praying always with all prayer and supplication
in the Spirit, and watching thereunto with all
perseverance and supplication for all the saints.
- Ephesians 6:18

One of Paul's duties and delights was in the area of prayer. First in Paul's prayer life was the importance of praying for those in positions of authority so the church could live a quiet and peaceable life (1 Timothy 2:1-2). According to Ephesians 6:18, there are all kinds of prayer for different purposes that can be used by the direction of the Holy Spirit. In studying his writings you see that each letter contains one or more prayers that he is praying for the churches or saints. These are post-resurrection prayers that can be used by all believers. They are especially effective when they are made personal or prayed for others. Note the prayers of Paul at the end of this section.

189

Paul's prayers were seasoned with praise and song and you can see in Acts 16 how, when he and Silas were imprisoned, they prayed and sang praises with a loud voice until the earth shook the prison doors open! He mentions singing in the Spirit in both Ephesians and Colossians.

PRAYER IN THE SPIRIT

We know that Paul was baptized in the Holy Spirit, used this prayer language frequently and also functioned in the gifts of the Spirit. In the book of 1 Corinthians 14, he talks much about prayer in tongues or in the Spirit. He contrasts the two, explaining the need for both and the place they should have in personal prayer and public gatherings.

> *For he that speaketh in an unknown tongue, speaketh not unto men but unto God: for no man understandeth him; howbeit in the spirit he speaketh mysteries.*
>
> *- 1 Corinthians 14:2*

> *He that speaketh in an unknown tongue edifieth himself....*
>
> *- 1 Corinthians 14:4*

For if I pray in an unknown tongue, my spirit prayeth, but my understanding is unfruitful. What is it then? I will pray with the spirit, and I will pray with the understanding also: I will sing with the spirit, and I will sing with the understanding also.

- 1 Corinthians 14:14, 15

I thank my God I speak with tongues more than ye all.

- 1 Corinthians 14:18

These are some examples of his use of speaking in tongues. As you study this chapter you see that he did not minimize its importance, but gave instruction for the sake of order in public meetings. A good example of this kind of prayer is in Acts 13 when certain prophets and teachers gathered for the purpose of fasting and ministering to the Lord. In that atmosphere of prayer, the Holy Spirit, spoke and gave them instruction concerning the ministry of Saul, as he was called at the time, and Barnabas. They were separated and sent out to fulfill a new assignment. He depended on prayer in the Spirit to pray the will of God (Romans 8:25, 26) and to cause doors of utterance to open (Colossians 4:3; Ephesians 6:19). Paul coveted the supply of Spirit of Jesus Christ given by the church in Philippi (Philippians 1:19).

Staying in an attitude of prayer will also help you to be led supernaturally like Paul when he had a vision of the man in Macedonia asking him to come (Acts 16:9,10). He was alert and steadfast in his prayer life, with thanksgiving (Colossians 4:2). He was a man of prayer who instructed us to pray about everything and follow through with thanksgiving to receive the supernatural (Philippians 4:6, 7).

My mother was a woman of much prayer. Some say I taught her how to pray! One night when I was a teenager, not living for God, I was with some boys in their car and was involved in a car wreck which totaled six cars. I thought, "This is how people die!" I walked out without a scratch and went home to find my mom sitting in her rocking chair praying. I told her what happened and she said, "I know. I have been praying for you and the Holy Spirit told me to tell you that Satan has desired to have you, so that he might sift you as wheat, but he won't because I have prayed for you." These are the same words Jesus told Peter in Luke 22:31,32. We must have this kind of prayer like Paul mentioned in Galatians 4:19 where he travailed in prayer until Christ was formed in the believers.

Here are some of the prayers Paul prayed that we can use to pray effectually for ourselves or for others.

192

EPHESIANS 1:17-23

That the God of our Lord Jesus Christ, the Father of glory, may give unto you the spirit of wisdom and revelation in the knowledge of him: The eyes of your understanding being enlightened; that ye may know what is the hope of his calling, and what the riches of the glory of his inheritance in the saints, And what is the exceeding greatness of his power to us-ward who believe, according to the working of his mighty power, Which he wrought in Christ, when he raised him from the dead, and set him at his own right hand in the heavenly places, Far above all principality, and power, and might, and dominion, and every name that is named, not only in this world, but also in that which is to come: And hath put all things under his feet, and gave him to be the head over all things to the church, Which is his body, the fullness of him that filleth all in all.

EPHESIANS 3:14-21

For this cause I bow my knees unto the Father of our Lord Jesus Christ, Of whom the whole family in heaven and earth is named, That he would grant you, according to the riches of his glory, to be strengthened with might by his Spirit in the inner man; That Christ may dwell in your hearts by faith; that ye, being rooted and grounded in love, May be able to comprehend with all saints what is the breadth, and length, and depth, and height; And to know the love of Christ, which passeth knowledge, that ye might be filled with all the fulness of God. Now unto him that is able to do exceeding abundantly above all that we ask or think, according to the power that worketh in us, Unto him be glory in the church by Christ Jesus throughout all ages, world without end. Amen.

COLOSSIANS 1:9-12

For this cause we also, since the day we heard it, do not cease to pray for you, and to desire that ye might be filled with the knowledge of his will in all wisdom and spiritual understanding; That ye might walk worthy of the Lord unto all pleasing, being fruitful in every good work, and increasing in the knowledge of God; Strengthened with all might, according to his glorious power, unto all patience and longsuffering with joyfulness; Giving thanks unto the Father, which hath made us meet to be partakers of the inheritance of the saints in light.

PHILIPPIANS 1:9-11

And this I pray, that your love may abound yet more and more in knowledge and in all judgment; That ye may approve things that are excellent; that ye may be sincere and without offense till the day of Christ. Being filled with the fruits of righteousness, which are by Jesus Christ, unto the glory and praise of God.

PHILEMON 4-6

I thank my God, making mention of thee always in my prayers, Hearing of thy love and faith, which thou hast toward the Lord Jesus, and toward all saints; That the communication of thy faith may become effectual by the acknowledging of every good thing which is in you in Christ Jesus.

1 THESSALONIANS 2:13

For this cause also thank we God without ceasing, because, when ye received the word of God which ye heard of us, ye received it not as the word of men, but as it is in truth, the word of God, which effectually worketh also in you that believe.

1 THESSALONIANS 5:23-24

And the very God of peace sanctify you wholly; and I pray God your whole spirit and soul and body be preserved blameless unto the coming of our Lord Jesus Christ. Faithful is he that calleth you, who also will do it.

Below you will find more references that contain prayers Paul prayed in his letters:

2 Timothy 4:16-18

1 Thessalonians 1:2-4

1 Thessalonians 3:11-13

2 Thessalonians 1:11-12

2 Thessalonians 2:16-17

S E C T I O N   T H R E E
TAKING YOUR PLACE IN THE BODY OF CHRIST

Probably the greatest satisfaction we get as believers after we are born again, is from being in our place, functioning and serving in our place in the Body of Christ. The epistles of Paul not only reveal the revelation of redemption but the bulk of them deal with our relationships and attitudes and how to function in the Church. The Lord said this to me years ago, "**The blessing and the move of God does not come by studying it alone, it comes by serving it.**"

THE BLESSING AND THE MOVE OF GOD DOES NOT COME BY STUDYING IT ALONE, IT COMES BY SERVING IT.

In Acts 9, the guys who were holding the rope for the Apostle Paul when he was let down in a basket outside the city wall probably didn't realize they are holding half of the New Testament in their hands.

The body of Christ cannot function unless it is assembled together. Look here at this scripture in Acts:

197

> *And when they had prayed, the place was shaken*
> *where they were assembled together; and they*
> *were all filled with the Holy Ghost, and they*
> *spake the word of God with boldness.*
>
> *- Acts 4:31*

Did you know that one of the key words in the book of Acts is the word "assembled?" Why did they assemble themselves? The body of Christ requires assembly. Have you ever bought your child a toy, maybe a bicycle or a tricycle or something for your baby? On the box it has a beautiful picture, but in fine print it says "some assembly required."

God says redemption is yours, blessing and healing is yours. He will show you a beautiful picture, but right at the bottom it says, "some assembly required." There is no other way to enjoy the benefits of the picture without each part getting in its place because some assembly is required. The Holy Spirit said it to me this way, "There are things you need to know that I am not going to tell you if I already told it to someone you are supposed to be in relationship with."

> *When he [Jesus] ascended up on high, he led*
> *captivity captive, and gave gifts unto men. And*
> *he gave some, apostles; and some, prophets; and*

some, evangelists; and some, pastors and teachers; For the perfecting of the saints, for the work of the ministry, for the edifying of the body of Christ: Till we all come in the unity of the faith, and of the knowledge of the Son of God, unto a perfect man, unto the measure of the stature of the fulness of Christ.

- Ephesians 4:8, 11-13

You have now yielded a hearty obedience to that system of truth in which you have been instructed.

- Romans 6:17 Weymouth

They were obedient to a form of doctrine that set them free from sin. As a Christian, when you submit to a pastor or other leaders in the church, you will be in a safe environment to become a disciple, be instructed in doctrine and changed in lifestyle. You will be equipped for functioning in your place in the Body of Christ.

Paul lived as an example, instructor and a spiritual father. He was an example of how to work hard and to suffer persecution and misunderstanding and the godly response to have. A good father has such a close relationship to his children that he can not only instruct, but discipline, bring correction and warning. Many do not want this kind of relationship today, but when Paul wrote First Corinthians he dealt with the same issues.

> *We work wearily with our own hands to earn our living. We bless those who curse us. We are patient with those who abuse us. We appeal gently when evil things are said about us. Yet we are treated like everybody's trash - right up to the present moment. I am not writing these things to shame you, but to warn you as my beloved children. For even if you had ten thousand others to teach you about Christ, you have only one spiritual father. For I became your father in Christ when I preached the Good News to you. So I urge you to imitate me.*
>
> *- 1 Corinthians 4:12-16 TLB*

Paul preached, warned, and instructed for the purpose that he may present every person mature (full-grown, fully initiated, complete and perfect) in Christ (Colossians 1:28, AMP). In Heaven, Jesus is praying and watching His Word to perform it. The Father God is working in us both to will and to do of his good pleasure. The Holy Spirit has been sent to be our Teacher, our Helper and give us revelation in the knowledge of God and perfecting what concerns us! He wants us to grow up to look like Him!

When I was a young boy, our family would go on vacations and stay in a cabin. One of the things I remember about the old camp house we stayed in was the marks on the wall that recorded the height of the children who had lived there. You could tell just how much taller each child had grown each year. I thought that might be what God does with each of His children. He wants us to grow and mature, but some of His kids might stay the same year after year or might even get shorter! When we are in our place in the Body of Christ and grow by hearing and doing the Word, there is a reward for diligence and it is evident to those around us.

> *But now put away and rid yourselves completely of all these things: anger, rage, bad feeling toward others, curses, slander, and foul-mouthed abuse and shameful utterances from your lips! Do not lie to one another, for you have stripped off the old (unregenerate) self with its evil practices, and have clothed yourselves with the new [spiritual self], which is [ever in the process of being] renewed and remolded into [fuller and more perfect knowledge upon]*

201

> *knowledge after the image (the likeness) of Him*
> *Who created it.*
>
> *- Colossians 3:8-10 Amplified*

In school there is a period of time when you are instructed. It is followed by tests which have to be studied for and passed before you go on to the next level of learning. Two important tests in the school of the Holy Spirit are the money test and the love test. The Holy Spirit is so patient and knows how to teach each one of His students so that they can pass if we just don't give up and quit. He will encourage us and give us strength to finish the courses with joy!

PASSING THE MONEY TEST

Paul set a standard for hard work, generous giving, sowing and reaping and reminded the churches to remember the words of Jesus, "It is more blessed to give than to receive," Acts 20:35. In 2 Corinthians 8-9 there is a pattern of how an individual or a church body gave out of their poverty until they always at all times had all sufficiency to give generously to every good work (2 Corinthians 9:8). He commanded and urged generosity and continued sowing and reaping financially in Galatians 6:6-10. He taught that you could open a debit and credit account in the kingdom of God through tithing and giving so that fruit would abound to your account. This would be a fragrant sacrifice to God and He would supply all your needs according to His riches in glory by Christ Jesus (Philippians 4:15-19). As a Christian and leader in the church it was important to him to teach the church to follow his example in giving, which was his obedience to the teaching of Jesus Christ.

> *Here's the lesson: Use your worldly resources to benefit others and make friends. Then, when your earthly possessions are gone, they will welcome you to an eternal home. If you are faithful in little things, you will be faithful in large ones. But if you are dishonest in little things, you won't be honest with greater responsibilities. And if you are untrustworthy about worldly wealth, who will trust you with the true riches of heaven? And if you are not faithful with other people's things, why should you be trusted with things of your own? No one can serve two masters. For you will hate the one and love the other; you will be devoted to one and despise the other. You cannot serve both God and money.*
>
> *- Luke 16:9-13 NLT*

The spirit of generosity is a defining mark of a Christian. Paul challenged the churches in his letters to follow his example in giving. The standard is set by Jesus Christ Himself. The grace of Jesus is that He became poor, so that we through His poverty could be made rich (2 Corinthians 8:9). This is part of His substitutionary work in redemption. In Galatians 3:13,14, Paul teaches us that Christ became a curse for us on the cross, so that the blessing of Abraham might come on the Gentiles through faith. As we give to others, Paul taught the church at Ephesus that whatever good thing they did, they would receive your reward from the Lord, no matter who you are (Ephesians 6:8).

WHEN YOU WANT WHAT GOD WANTS FOR THE SAME REASON HE WANTS IT, YOU ARE INVINCIBLE.

This matter of giving and receiving was so important to Paul and such a part of the New Testament church that Paul left Titus in Corinth to specifically teach them about this grace of giving and receiving (2 Corinthians 8:6). Through this ministry there were needs met and the blessing of God came upon the churches and individuals, the same as in Acts 2:45 and 4:34,35. When Christians grow up in this area of giving and receiving, there is abundance and supply, freedom from the love of money and the churches are strong! There is no end to the blessing of God. "When you want what God wants for the same reason He wants it, you are invincible (F.F. Bosworth)."

PASSING THE LOVE TEST

First and Second Timothy and Philemon are rich in instructions to those in the five fold ministry. They contain specific guidelines concerning holy conduct, church affairs, and exhortations to be bold and on fire with the gift of God. Very essential to the work of God is harmony and unity among Christians. Over time, the love of God became Paul's quest and its importance grew as Paul became more acquainted with Christ Jesus.

My daddy would always say, "You can tell how you are getting along with God by how people look to you!" I learned that even though I had a gift or anointing it was of no use to the Body of Christ if my attitude was wrong or I held offense against others.

I remember one times when Bro. Hagin was preaching on walking in love. I swallowed my pride, made some adjustments and repented. Just a few weeks later I had a great financial breaktrough.

Relationships are key to the personal growth and the entire advance of the kingdom of God. As a young pastor I was zealous to make progress in the first little church I pastored. One of the members was giving me trouble and I knew I could straighten him out! There was a district superintendent of my denomination who I liked to spend time with and I told him about this particular issue in my church. This wise elder gave me some of the best advice - I will never forget that day. He said, "Mark, you may be able to whip a skunk, but you might not want to!" That slowed me down and realized I should pray about things, get the wisdom of God and release the care of them to God and He would fight my battles for me! That is walking in love. I learned to be quick to repent, quick to forgive and quick to believe. When you practice the love of God, you will grow up.

YOU CAN TELL HOW YOU ARE GETTING ALONG WITH GOD BY HOW PEOPLE LOOK TO YOU!   - B.B HANKINS

Ephesians 5:1,2 (Amplified) says, "Therefore be imitators of God [copy Him and follow His example], as well-beloved children [imitate their father]. And walk in love, [esteeming and delighting in one another]...." When you walk in love, you will be honest and will glorify God in all your relationships doing nothing to discredit the name of

Jesus and the work of God.

Another lesson I learned as a young husband is that if I wanted God to answer my prayers, I needed to treat my wife right, walking in love with her. One time I was praying and the Lord spoke to me, telling me He would not hear me until I made things right with Trina. Talk about crucifying the flesh! I had to apologize and only then I felt the presence of the Lord as I went to pray (1 Peter 3:7).

Bro. Hagin said that walking in love is the way to victory, and it is the truth! If you walk in love you will display all the fruit of the spirit and not fulfill the lusts of the flesh (Galatians 5:19-23). The love of God is released into our spirits by the Holy Spirit (Romans 5:8). When we follow after it, the gifts of the Spirit will begin to flow and Paul told us to eagerly pursue and seek to acquire this love and to make it our great quest (1 Corinthians 14:1 Amplified).

YOU MAY BE ABLE TO WHIP A SKUNK, BUT YOU MAY NOT WANT TO.

THE LOVE OF GOD

If I can speak in the tongues of men and even of angels, but have not love, I am only a noisy gong or a clanging cymbal. And if I have prophetic powers, and understand all the secret truths and mysteries and possess all knowledge, and if I have sufficient faith so that I can remove mountains, but have not love (God's love in me) I am nothing (a useless nobody). Even if I dole out all that I have [to the poor in providing] food, and if I surrender my body to be burned, but have not love (God's love in me), I gain nothing. Love endures long and is patient and kind; love never is envious nor boils over with jealousy, is not boastful or vainglorious, does not display itself haughtily. It is not conceited (arrogant and inflated with pride); it is not rude (unmannerly) and does not act unbecomingly. Love (God's love in us does not insist on its own rights or its own way, for it is not self-seeking; it is not touchy or fretful or resentful; it takes no account of the evil done to it [it pays no attention to a suffered wrong]. It does not rejoice in injustice and unrighteousness, but rejoices when right and truth prevail. Love bears up under anything and everything that comes, is ever ready to believe the best of every person, its hopes are fadeless under all circumstances, and it endures everything [without weakening]. Love never fails [never fades out or becomes obsolete or comes to an end].

- 1 Corinthians 13:1-8 (Amplified)

There is only one standard of perfection and that is Jesus Christ. Through our identification with Him in His death, burial and resurrection; who we are and what we have now in Christ; through the power of the Holy Spirit working in us; and what Jesus is doing for us now in Heaven, we can grow up into Christ in all things. Instead of being tossed about by different winds of doctrine and trends of the day, we can grow up into the full stature of Christ by taking our place in Him.

> *Being confident of this very thing, that he which hath begun a good work in you will perform it until the day of Jesus Christ.*
>
> *- Philippians 1:6*

Study Questions

<u>CHAPTER 1</u>
THE LIFE OF PAUL: THE TRAJECTORY OF FAITH

1. The word _____also means a chosen or taken path.

2. The word trajectory is defined in Webster's dictionary as the path followed by an _____

_____

3. _____refers to himself as a "man in Christ" in 2 Corinthians 12:2.

4. Write Galatians 2:20

_____
_____
_____
_____
_____

5. Write Ephesians 2:6

_____
_____
_____
_____
_____

6. Believers are alive not just on the earth, but also in _____ by virtue of being _____.

7. What God did in Christ was for the _____ and _____.

8. The Lord Jesus Christ used Paul to _____ the way and to draw the map that believers walk today in Christ.

9. The letters of Paul are divinely inspired, and rich in deepest spiritual truths, are the advanced _____ of our Lord Jesus Christ.

10. Write Acts 20:24

_____

_____

_____

_____

_____

11. Write Acts 26:2

_____

_____

_____

_____

_____

CHAPTER 2
THE CENTER OF THE GOSPEL

1. The four Gospels – Matthew, Mark, Luke and John – are a _____ of the Gospel, the book of Acts is a _____ of the Gospel; and Paul's letters are an _____ of the Gospel.

2. The four Gospels tell what _____ saw; Paul's epistles tell what _____ saw.

3. The center of the _____ is what God has done for you in Christ in His death, burial, and resurrection.

4. Write 2 Timothy 1:13 in The Living Bible

_____

_____

_____

_____

_____

5. Write Romans 6:17, Weymouth

_____

_____

_____

_____

_____

6. Write John 8:32, 36

_____

_____

_____

_____

_____

7. The first system that was established (Hebrews 9-10) has been replaced with a new and _____ system ordained by God and sealed by the _____.

8. James Stalker said, "Paul's letters contain the _____ that Jesus carried away from this world unuttered."

9. The Apostle Paul's letters contain an inter-dependent group of _____ that came from what God has done for us in Christ.

10. This system of _____ centers on the death, burial, and resurrection of Christ with the restoration of man as the _____.

<u>Name the 8 Points of Paul's System of Truth</u>

11. _____

12. _____

13. _____

14. _____

15. _____

16. _____

17. _____

18. _____

CHAPTER 3: POINT 1 - PAUL'S PNEUMA CONCEPT

1. Write Psalm 8:4-6

_____

_____

_____

_____

_____

_____

2. Write Genesis 1:26

_____

_____

_____

_____

3. Write 1 Thessalonians 5:23

_____

_____

_____

_____

4. The Greek word for "spirit" is _____.

5. You are a _____, with a _____ (which includes your mind, will, and emotions), and you are staying in a _____ (the house you live in).

6. Paul's letters are centered on the fact that the real you is a _____ not a _____.

7. When you are born again or saved, your _____ (spirit) is born again, hooked up to _____ (Romans 8:2).

8. As the _____feeds your spirit, your inward man will rise up and take _____ over your body and mind.

9. Write Colossians 1:13, KJV

_____
_____
_____
_____
_____
_____

10. Write Colossians 1:13, Jordan

_____
_____
_____
_____
_____
_____

11. Write Philippians 3:3

_____
_____
_____
_____
_____

12. Write Romans 8:7

_____

_____

_____

_____

_____

13. When you are born again, your _____ (inward man) is joined to Christ and becomes a new creation.

14. Man is a _____, he has a _____, and he lives in a _____.

15. God expects you to get your body and soul in subjection to your spirit man by availing yourself to His_____ and His _____ (2 Corinthians 4:16).

CHAPTER 4
POINT 2 - MAN'S IDENTIFICATION WITH ADAM

1. Everyone in the entire human race originated from the Garden of Eden out of the first man, _____, and his wife, _____.

2. You were not born in the condition Adam was created in; you were born in the condition he _____.

3. We were born, not in the _____ that God created Adam, but in the condition caused by Adam's sin.

4. Adam, now a blemished "_____," produced and duplicated the same blemish in every _____ that was ever born.

5. The same law that allowed one man to affect every man is the same law that allowed Jesus Christ, the last Adam, to take the first Adam's condition of sin, the _____, _____, and _____.

6. The whole Bible is really about two men: the _____ Adam and the _____ Adam.

7. There is no hope for man's _____ without Jesus Christ.

8. Once we are born again, we are no longer _____ to sin.

9. The power of _____ will make you free from sin.

10. Write Romans 8:1-2

_____
_____
_____
_____
_____

CHAPTER 5
POINT 3 - MAN'S CONDITION IN ADAM

1. In his alienation and separation from God, Adam actually became an _____ of God.

2. The shedding of _____ was always required for the _____ of sins.

3. Job gives revelation of man's _____ and _____ in this world.

4. There are three major revelations from the book of Job: _____, _____, and _____.

5. Write Romans 3:9,10

_____

_____

_____

_____

_____

6. Write Ephesians 2:1,2, Phillips

_____

_____

_____

_____

_____

_____

7. When you follow the course of this world, the prince of the power of the air – the spirit that works in the children of disobedience – _____.

8. The word "_____" in Ephesians 2:4-7 means "He has given us life – spiritual life."

9. This life restores dominion to the point that we are no longer controlled by our _____ or our

_____.

10. Paul told us to be thankful to God for all things: thankful for giving us the _____; thankful for always causing us to _____; thankful for _____ us for our inheritance in Christ; thankful for _____ from the power of darkness and for _____ us into the kingdom of His dear Son.

11. In Christ, you have _____ through His blood, even the _____ of sin.

12. Everything we need pertaining to _____ and _____ has been provided in Christ (2 Peter 1:3).

CHAPTER 6: POINT 4 - WHAT HAPPENED TO JESUS FROM THE CROSS TO THE THRONE

1. Write Hebrews 9:12, Amplified

_____

_____

_____

_____

_____

2. Write Ephesians 1:7

_____

_____

_____

_____

_____

3. Write Colossians 1:14

_____

_____

_____

_____

_____

4. Write Galatians 3:13

_____

_____

_____

_____

_____

5. _____ simply means freedom or deliverance through the payment of a price.

6. Jesus did not die the death of a martyr; he died as our

_____

7. Write John 18:37

_____
_____
_____
_____

8. Write Revelation 13:8

_____
_____
_____
_____

9. Write John 10:17,18

_____
_____
_____
_____

10. Write 2 Corinthians 5:17, Amplified

_____
_____
_____
_____

11. Write Isaiah 53:4,5

_____
_____
_____
_____

12. On the cross, Jesus became our substitute for the
_____ of sin.

13. Jesus took the punishment that we deserved and
redeemed us from_____.

14. Jesus was the first man to enter the death experience and _____ it.

15. Jesus destroyed the _____, put him to _____, and _____ him.

CHAPTER 7:
POINT 5 - YOUR IDENTIFICATION WITH CHRIST

1. Define "identification": _____
_____
_____

2. The glory and the mystery of the believer's life is that he or she is _____ with the master – _____ from Him.

3. In His _____ and _____, Jesus went to the headquarters of evil and took care of evil for every person for all time.

4. Jesus became a man so the _____ He accomplished could be obtained by everyone.

5. Let the Word of God establish your _____.

6. Write 2 Corinthians 5:14 Laubach Translation
_____
_____
_____
_____
_____

7. Write Romans 6:6
_____
_____
_____
_____
_____

8. Write Romans 6:11

_____
_____
_____
_____

9. Write Galatians 6:14

_____
_____
_____
_____

10. Write Galatians 2:20 - Distilled

_____
_____
_____
_____
_____

CHAPTER 8: POINT 6 - WHO WE ARE AND WHAT WE HAVE NOW IN CHRIST

1. Write 2 Corinthians 5:17 (Amlified)

_____
_____
_____
_____
_____

2. God did _____ what He wanted to do in everyman.

3. God's work in Christ far outweighs anything done to us by _____

4.　Everything God did for us in Christ is
_____ of our account.

5. Name four phrases that describe your position after the new birth _____.

6. Write 1 Corinthians 1:30

_____
_____
_____
_____
_____

7. Write Colossians 2:9-10

_____
_____
_____
_____
_____

8. Write 2 Corintians 5:21

_____
_____
_____
_____
_____

9. Write Colossians 2:3

_____
_____
_____
_____
_____

10.　The central theme of the Gospel of John is
_____.

11. Eternal Life is the _____ of God. It is a spiritual substance that is in God.

12. Write 1 John 5:4

_____

_____

_____

_____

13. In Matthew, Mark, and Luke - the main theme is the

_____.

14. Write Colossians 1:13

_____

_____

_____

_____

_____

15. The kingdom of God is _____, _____, and _____ in the Holy Ghost.

CHAPTER 9: POINT 7 - WHAT JESUS IS DOING FOR US NOW

1. There is an eternal union between God and man because Jesus fully _____ with us.

2. Jesus, according to the perfect will of God, is still actively working for our good to save us to the _____ by ever living to make for us.

3. Write Hebrews 8:6

_____

_____

_____

_____

_____

4. Jesus fulfilled every detail of the new covenant and with His _____, _____ and _____ activated the new will and testament forever.

5. Write Hebrew 7:22

_____
_____
_____
_____
_____

6. Write Hebrews 7:25

_____
_____
_____
_____
_____

7. The word *save* or *salvation* in the Greek is the same word as _____

_____.

8. Write Romans 8:34

_____
_____
_____
_____
_____

9. The Greek word for _____ is antidikos, which simply means a lawyer who argues in court or it means a

_____.

10. Write 1 John 2:1

_____
_____
_____
_____

11. Jesus can only do his job when we say something. He represents our _____ before the Father God.

12. Write Hebrews 13:20, 21

_____

_____

_____

_____

_____

CHAPTER 10: POINT 8 -
HOW TO GROW UP IN CHRIST

SECTION 1
1. Write Colossians 2:6-7

_____

_____

_____

_____

_____

2. Write Romans 12:1-2

_____

_____

_____

_____

_____

3. The _____ of your mind is a continual, lifetime process.

4. You are to reckon that you _____ with Christ, were _____ with Him, and were _____ with Him. Then sin shall no longer have _____ over you.

5. The _____ breaks the control of the enemy, but you still have to recieve the _____ which is able to save your soul.

6. The Word says, "Jesus gave Himself for us to redeem us from all _____." (Titus 2:14)

7. Write 2 Corinthians 10:4-5

_____

_____

_____

_____

_____

8. Write 1 Timothy 4:15

_____

_____

_____

_____

_____

9. _____ is a relationship with the Word of God.

SECTION 2
10. Write Ephesians 6:18

_____

_____

_____

_____

_____

11. Write 1 Corinthians 14:2

_____

_____

_____

_____

_____

12. Write 1 Corinthians 14:4

_____

_____

_____

_____

_____

13. Paul depended on prayer in the Spirit to pray_____ and to cause _____ to open.

14. We must have the kind of prayer like Paul mentioned in _____ where he travailed in prayer until Christ was formed in the believers.

SECTION 3

15. The blessing and the move of God does not come by _____ it alone, it comes by _____ it.

16. Write Acts 4:31

_____

_____

_____

_____

_____

17. The body of Christ cannot function unless it is
_____ together.

18. Write Colossians 3:8 (Amplified)

_____

_____

_____

_____

_____

19. Luke 16 tells us if we are _____ in little
things, you will be faithful in large things.

20. When you want what _____ wants for
the same reason He wants it, you are
_____.

21. Write Ephesians 5:1-2 (Amplified)

_____

_____

_____

_____

_____

22. If you _____ in the spirit you will not
_____ the lust of the flesh.

23. Write Romans 5:8

_____

_____

_____

_____

_____

ANSWER KEY FOR STUDY QUESTIONS

CHAPTER 1:
1. trajectory
2. object moving through space, also a chosen or taken path.
3. The Apostle Paul
4. Galatians 2:20
5. Ephesians 2:6
6. Heaven, In Christ
7. whole world, every generation
8. pioneer
9. teachings
10. Acts 20:24
11. Acts 26:2

CHAPTER 2
1. proclamation, demonstration, explanation
2. man, God
3. Gospel
4. 2 Timothy 1:13
5. Romans 6:17, Weymouth
6. John 8:32, 36
7. better, blood of His Son, Jesus Christ.
8. thoughts
9. revelation realities
10. truth, object
11. Paul's Pneuma Concept: Spirit, Soul, and Body
12. Identification with Adam
13. Man's Condition in Adam
14. What happened to Jesus – from the Cross to the Throne
15. Identification with Christ
16. Who we are and what we have NOW in Christ
17. What Jesus is doing for us NOW
18. How to Grow Up in Christ

231

CHAPTER 3

1. Psalm 8:4-6
2. Genesis 1:26
3. 1 Thessalonians 5:23
4. pneuma
5. spirit, soul, body
6. spirit, body
7. pneuma, God
8. Word, dominion
9. Colossians 1:13, KJV
10. Colossians 1:13, Jordan
11. Philippians 3:3
12. Romans 8:7
13. spirit
14. spirit, soul, body
15 Holy Spirit, Word

CHAPTER 4

1. Adam, Eve
2. Passed on
3. condition
4. master, copy
5. curse, shame, and death.
6. first, last
7. condition
8. slaves
9. righteousness
10. Romans 8:1-2

CHAPTER 5

1. enemy

2. blood, atonement

3. experience, condition

4. man needs righteousness, man needs a revelation of God, and man needs a mediator and a redeemer.

5. Romans 3:9,10

6. Ephesians 2:1,2, Phillips

7. controls you

8. quickens

9. flesh, mind

10. victory, triumph, qualifying, delivering, translating

11. redemption, forgiveness

12. life, godliness

CHAPTER 6

1. Hebrews 9:12, Amplified

2. Ephesians 1:7

3. Colossians 1:14

4. Galatians 3:13

5. Redemption

6. substitute

7. John 18:37

8. Revelation 13:8

9. John 10:17,18

10. 2 Corinthians 5:17, Amplified

11. Isaiah 53:4,5

12. penalty

13. the curse of the law.

14. master

15. devil, naught, paralyzed him.

CHAPTER 7

1. to consider or treat as the same, the condition or fact of being, the same in all qualities under consideration.
2. one, inseparable .
3. death, resurrection,
4. victory
5. identity.
6. 2 Corinthians 5:14 Laubach Translation
7. Romans 6:6
8. Romans 6:11
9. Galatians 6:14
10. Galatians 2:20 - Distilled

CHAPTER 8

1. 2 Corinthians 5:17
2. In Christ
3. Adams Fall.
4. set to the credit
5. In Christ, In Whom, In the Lord, In Him
6. 1 Corinthians 1:30
7. Colossians 2:9-10
8. 2 Corintians 5:21
9. Colossians 2:3
10. eternal life.
11. divine nature
12. 1 John 5:4
13. Kingdom of God.
14. Colossians 1:13
15. righteousness, peace, joy

CHAPTER 9

1. identified

2. uttermost
3. Hebrews 8:6
4. death, burial resurrection
5. Hebrew 7:22
6. Hebrews 7:25
7. deliverance, safety, healing, preservation soundness.
8. Romans 8:34
9. adversary prosecutor.
10. 1 John 2:1
11. confession
12. Hebrews 13:20, 21

CHAPTER 10

SECTION 1

1. Colossians 2:6-7
2. Romans 12:1-2
3. renewing
4. died, buried, raised, dominion
5. anointing, engrafted Word
6. iniquity.
7. 2 Corinthians 10:4-5
8. 1 Timothy 4:15
9. Meditation

SECTION 2

10. Ephesians 6:18
11. 1 Corinthians 14:2
12. 1 Corinthians 14:4
13. the will of God, doors of utterance
14. Galatians 4:19

<u>SECTION 3</u>
15. studying, serving it.
16. Acts 4:31
17. assembled
18. Colossians 3:8 (Amplified)
19. faithful
20. God invincible.
21. Ephesians 5:1-2 (Amplified)
22. walk, fulfill
23. Romans 5:8

CONFESSION OF WHO YOU ARE IN CHRIST

That the communication of thy faith may become effectual by the acknowledging of every good thing which is in you in Christ Jesus.

- Philemon 6

I am a new creation in Christ. Old things are passed away, and everything has become new. I forget the past. I am new — a new person, with new life, in a new kingdom in Christ Jesus. The dominion of God, the move of God and the realm of God are within me. I have been delivered from the power of darkness and Satan's authority, and translated into the kingdom of the Son of God. I am in that kingdom right now. I have entered into the realm of God. I can see things with my spiritual eyes in the Word and by the Holy Spirit, so I boldly declare that I am in Christ and in the kingdom. Righteousness, peace, and joy in the Holy Ghost are mine in Christ. In the kingdom I have been made righteous. I have the peace of God. I have the joy of the Lord. I have the Holy Ghost. The Spirit of God is my Helper and Teacher.

All things are possible to him who believes. I am who God says I am. I have been redeemed. I am in Him, and He is in me. I am saved. I have been born of God. Whoever is born of God overcomes the world, and this is the victory, even my faith. In Christ I am victorious, I am blessed and I have redemption. I can do what God says I can do. I know there are giants in the land, but I walk by faith and not by sight. I see the unseen. God's movement, ability, and power are in me and available to me. I can do all things through Christ who strengthens me. Devil, you are a liar. You are under my feet. Your power is broken over my family and my future. I submit to You, Father. As I resist the devil, he runs from me. I submit to the Word. I agree with the Word. Devil, take your hands off my mind, my body, and my finances, in Jesus' name. I belong to God. I hold fast to my confession of faith. I am blessed so I can be a blessing around the world. I can see there is a highway and there is traffic from Heaven to my house. By the blood of Jesus I am redeemed. Thank You, Father God, for redeeming me. Thank You for Your mercy and grace. I reign as a king in life through Jesus Christ. I am seated with Christ in heavenly places. He whom the Son sets free is free indeed. I mix faith with the Word of God. Victory is mine. The blessing of the Lord is mine. Thank

You, Lord, that I have all that You say that I have. Thank You, Lord, that You supply all my needs. Lord, because You are my Shepherd, I shall not want. You have prepared a table before me in the presence of my enemies. Right now I am eating from the righteousness, the redemption, the healing, the victory, the joy, and the peace. Thank You, Father, that it is mine in Christ. Thank You, Lord, for the reality of redemption. Blessing is mine now. Healing is mine now in Jesus' name. Strength is mine. I am strong in You, Lord, and in the power of Your might. Faith says it is mine now. Faith says what God says.

Purchasing and Contact Information

**Mark Hankins Ministries
PO Box 12863
Alexandria, LA 71315**

Phone: **318.448.4500**
Fax: **318.443.2948**

E-mail: **contact@markhankins.org**

Visit us on the web:

www.markhankins.org

Books by Mark Hankins

Spirit-Filled Scripture Study Guide - $35
This is a comprehensive study of scriptures in over 120 different translations covering many topics including redemption, faith, finances, and prayer.

The Spirit of Faith - $15
If you only knew what was on the other side of your mountian you would move it! Having a spirit of faith is necessary to do the will of God and fulfill your destiny. The Spirit of faith turns defeat into victory and dreams into reality.

The Bloodline of a Champion - $15
The blood of Jesus is "liquid love" that flows from the heart of God and gives us hope in all circumstances. In this book we will be studying the power of the blood of Jesus. Not only will we clearly see what the blood has done *for us*, but also what it does *in us* as believers.

Taking Your Place In Christ - $12.50
Many Christians talk about what they are trying to be and what they are going to be. This book is about who you are *now* as a believer in Christ.

Let the Good Times Roll - $12.50
This book focuses on the five keys to Heaven on earth: The Holy Spirit, glory, faith, joy, and redemption. The Holy Spirit is a genius. If you will listen to Him, He will make you look smart.

Revolutionary Revelation - $12.50

This book provides excellent insight on how the spirit of wisdom and revelation is mandatory for believers to access their call, inheritance, and authority in Christ.

The Power of Identification With Christ - $15

This book focuses on the reality of redemption and your new identity in Christ. As a new creature, you have everything you need inside of you to succeed in life!

Never Run at Your Giant With Your Mouth Shut - $5

When David ran at Goliath, there was a war of words going on. In this book, we learn that winning the war of words is necessary to winning the fight of faith.

11:23 - The Language of Faith - $12.50

Never understimate the power of one voice! This book contains over 100 inspirational, mountain moving quotes to "stir up" the spirit of faith in you.

Acknowledging Every Good Thing That Is In You In Christ - $2.50

This mini-book encourages every believer to have a daily confession or acknowledgment of who they are in Christ.

CD Series

Paul's System of Truth - 12 CD's

These CD's will give you an in depth look at Paul's Letters and the system of truth that reveals man's redemption.

For More Information:
www.markhankins.org

Mark and Trina Hankins travel nationally and internationally preaching the Word of God with the power of the Holy Spirit. Their message centers on the spirit of faith, the identify of the believer in Christ, and the work of the Holy Spirit.

After over 35 years of pastoral and traveling ministry, Mark and Trina are now ministering full-time in campmeetings, leadership conferences, and church services around the world and across the United States. Their son Aaron Hankins and his wife Errin Cody are now the pastors of Christian Worship Center in Alexandria, Louisiana. Their daughter Alica Moran and her husband Caleb pastor Metro Life Church in Lafayette, Louisiana. Mark and Trina also have five grandchildren.

Mark is also the author of several books. For more information on Mark Hankins Ministries please log on to our website, **www.markhankins.org.**

Acknowledgements

Special Thanks To:

My wife, Trina
My son, Aaron, and his wife Errin Cody
    Their children Avery Jane, Macy Claire, and
    Jude Aaron
My daughter, Alicia, and her husband Caleb
    Their children Jaiden Mark and Gavin Luke
My parents, Pastors B.B. and Velma Hankins, who are
    now in Heaven with the Lord
My wife's parents, Rev. William and Ginger Behrman

Reference Page

Amplified Bible. Zondervan Publishing House, Grand Rapids, Michigan, 1972.

Barclay, William. The New Testament, A New Translation. Collins, London, England, 1968.

Boorstin, Daniel. "History's Hidden Turning Points," US News and World Report, 22 April, 1991: 52.

Bruce, F.F. The Letters of Paul, An Expanded Paraphrase. Eerdmans Publishing Company, Grand Rapids, Michigan, 1965.

Carpenter, S.C. Selections from Romans and The Letter to the Philippians. Spirit to Spirit Publications, 1981.

Cressman, A. Good News for the World. Soon! Publications, Bombay, India, 1969.

Conybeare and Howson. The Life and Epistles of Paul.

Fenton, Ferrar, The Holy Bible in Modern English. Destiny Publisher, Massachusetts, n.d.

Good News Bible, The Bible in Today's English Version. American Bible Society, New York, New York, 1976.

Gordon, A.J. In Christ, or, the Believer's Union with His Lord. Gould and Lincoln, Boston, 1872.

Johnson, Ben Campbell. The Heart of Paul. A Rational Paraphrase of the New Testament. Word Books, Waco, Texas, 1976.

Jordan, Clarence. The Cotton Patch Version of Paul's Epistles. Association Press, New York, New York, 1968.

Knox, Ronald. The New Testament of Our Lord and Savior Jesus Christ, A New Translation. Sheed and Ward, New York, New York, 1953.

Laubach, Frank C. The Inspired Letters in Clearest English. Thomas Nelson and Sons, New York, New York, 1956.

Lovett, C.S. Lovett's Lights on Galatians, Ephesians, Philippians, Colossians, 1 & 2 Thessalonians with Rephrased Text. Personal Christianity, Baldwin Park, California, 1969.

Moffat, James. The Holy Bible Containing the Old and New Testaments. Double Day and Company, Inc., New York, New York, 1926.

Morris, Leon. The Cross and The New Testament. WM. E. Eerdmans Publishing, Grand Rapides/Cambridge, December 1, 1999.

Nelson, P.C. The Life of Paul. Gospel Publishing House, Springfield, Missouri, nd.

New English Bible. Oxford University Press, Oxford, England, 1961.

Noli, Fans. S. The New Testament of Our Lord and Savior Jesus Christ. Albanian Orthodox Church in America, Boston, Massachusetts, 1961.

Parshall, Gerald. "The Momentous Mission of the Apostle Paul," US News and World Report, 22 April, 1991: 54-55.

Phillips, J.B. The New Testament in Modern English. The Macmillan Company, New York, New York, 1958.

Richert, Ernest L. Freedom Dynamics. The Thinker, Big Bear Lake, California, 1977.

Rotherham, J.B. The Emphasized Bible. Kregel Publications, Grand Rapids, Michigan, 1976.

Schonfield, Hugh. The Authentic New Testament. Dennis Dobson, Ltd., Great Britian, 1955.

Stanley, Arthur. The Epistles of Paul in Modern English. Verploegh Editions, Wheaton, Illinois, 1980.

Stalker, James. The Life of St. Paul. The Zondervan Corporation, Grand Rapides, Michigan, 1984.

Taylor,Ken. The Living Bible. Tyndale House Publishers, Wheaton, Illinois, 1971.

The Distilled Bible/New Testament. Paul Benjamin Publishing Company. Stone Mountain, Georgia, 1980.

The Jerusalem Bible. Double Day and Company, Inc., New York, New York, 1968.

Way, Arthur S. The Letters of St. Paul to the Seven Churches and Three Friends with the Letter to the Hebrews, Sixth Edition. Macmillian and Company, New York, New York, 1926.

Webster, Noah. The American Dictionary of the English Language, 1828.

Weymouth, Richard Francis. The New Testament. James Clark and Company, London, England, 1909.

Wigglesworth, Smith. Ever Increasing Faith. Springfield, Missouri, Gospel Publishing House, 1996.

Wilson, Marvin. "The Apostle Paul and His Times: Did You Know". christianitytoday.com, Issue 47, 1995.

Verkuyl, Gerrit. The Holy Bible, The New Berkeley Version Revised Editions, in Modern English. Zondervan Publishing House, Grand Rapides, Michigan, 1969.

NOTES

NOTES